AS THEY GROW

# Pregnancy
## and
# Childbirth

AS THEY GROW

# Pregnancy
and
Childbirth

❦

**Paula Adams Hillard, M.D.
and Gideon G. Panter, M.D.**

**Edited by Dodi Schultz
and the Editors of *Parents*™**

**BALLANTINE BOOKS
NEW YORK**

# Contents

# Preface

❦

## Thinking about Being Pregnant

As an obstetrician, I play a unique role. Each of my patients is really *two* patients—the mother-to-be and the child growing and developing within her womb. And the medicine I practice is in very great part *preventive* medicine—not the treatment of illness (after all, pregnancy is not a disease but a normal condition) but continuing care that will prevent problems and assure the good health of both mother and child.

In this effort, I have a very important partner: the mother-to-be herself. In fact, ideally, she has assumed her responsibility in our partnership before she has come to my office and we have confirmed the fact of her pregnancy—and even before conception!

This responsibility consists, essentially, of providing the best possible prenatal environment, a setting in which her baby-to-be can best develop and thrive. The best environment is a body that is in the best possible health: It is a healthy mother who is most likely to have a healthy baby.

Some of the most important factors to think about, when you're thinking about being pregnant, involve habits and lifestyle.

One of those factors is nutrition. Pregnancy is often a powerful motivator. One of the most common changes I see women making when they find they are pregnant is that they pay attention to their diets. Women who subsisted chiefly on junk food, sodas, and sweets switch to more healthful foods and begin to consume vegetables, fruits, and calcium-rich foods to assure their babies' good bone development. They learn that marginal deficiencies of certain vitamins and minerals may be associated with some birth defects, and that many women have low resources of iron. They discuss their diets with their doctors and take supplementary vitamins or minerals if their dietary intake is found inadequate. (In pregnancy, supplementary iron is almost always recommended, and supplementary folic acid is sometimes routinely suggested as well.)

But why not think about good nutrition even before you're pregnant? You can make yourself a healthier person—and assure your baby of all the essentials from the very moment of conception.

Similarly, I find that many women are motivated by pregnancy to start toning up, to attend an exercise class or begin other regular physical activity. Many physicians feel that women who are physically fit have a lower risk of problems during pregnancy and labor (and most studies suggest that, for women who have no special medical problems, moderate exercise during pregnancy is not harmful). Again—why wait until you are pregnant?

These are positive steps you can take, healthful habits you can add to your lifestyle. There is also another area you should think about: *negative* parts of your lifestyle that may be harmful to your baby (even before you know you're pregnant) and may be harmful to *you*, as well—in particular, the use of (nonmedical) drugs, including alcoholic beverages.

There is a great deal of evidence that alcohol in large amounts is definitely harmful to the developing baby; regular consumption of medium to large amounts of alcoholic beverages can lead to lower birth weights and to growth deficiencies that may persist even after birth. Alcohol is one of the three leading causes of birth defects, and it is the only one in which such results are entirely preventable.

It is not known if there is any "safe" level of alcohol intake in pregnancy. The U.S. Surgeon General, in a statement published in 1981, advises women who are pregnant or considering pregnancy not to drink alcoholic beverages at all and to be aware of the alcohol content of foods and medications as well. It is clear that there is *no* risk of alcohol-related birth defects if the mother consumes *no* alcohol. It seems prudent for all women who are pregnant or attempting to conceive too assess their drinking habits honestly and realistically and to consider not drinking or at least curtailing their alcohol consumption.

How about caffeine? The studies of coffee and tea consumption and its effects in pregnancy have been contradictory. Most evidence suggests that moderate consumption has no adverse effects. But restricting the number of cups per day is probably a reasonable precaution for the woman who is pregnant or contemplating pregnancy.

As for tobacco, the evidence is quite clear: It is, as the legend on every pack of cigarettes warns, dangerous to your health. It is equally dangerous to the health of an unborn child. Smokers are more likely to have miscarriages. Babies born to smokers are smaller and more likely to be undernourished. There is an increased risk of premature birth and of such complications as bleeding and early separation of the placenta. There are higher rates of stillbirths and of newborn deaths in the offspring of mothers who smoke.

Quitting is not easy. But if you are pregnant or planning to become pregnant, it really is extremely important, for your child's sake as well as your own. As an American Cancer Society poster puts it, "Why start a life under a cloud?"

I am often asked about marijuana. Is it as dangerous as tobacco? My advise is simply this: We are sure that marijuana has no *beneficial* effects on a developing baby. We know that marijuana smoking, like cigarette smoking, can decrease the amount of oxygen reaching the baby, which can be harmful—and there *may* be other harmful effects as well. Like anything that could possibly interfere with the optimal health of your baby, it is best avoided.

If you are thinking about conceiving, you should also remember that many medications, while helpful to the person who is taking them, may adversely affect a developing baby. Many women are aware of this fact, and it's relatively common for me to receive a call from a woman whose menstrual period is two weeks late, who believes she might be pregnant, and who is very worried about the medication she has taken for a minor ailment, such as a cold or headache. Usually, I can reassure her that, as far as we know, that particular medication has no harmful effect—although, of course, I cannot offer a guarantee.

Most ordinary medications, such as aspirin and other over-the-counter antipain drugs, have not been shown to be harmful during pregnancy. A woman who is trying to conceive, however, should keep in mind the possibility that she may be pregnant, as well as the fact that early pregnancy is the time when the fetus is at highest risk of drug-caused birth defects. If you are pregnant or planning to conceive, it's best to avoid any unnecessary medications and to check with your doctor concerning any you feel are needed, whether prescription or nonprescription.

Finally—is a preconception visit to a physician a good idea? I think it is, for several reasons. Your medical history might suggest potential problems requiring further evaluation. Although it is unlikely, there may be indications that reproductive difficulties may arise, such as factors affecting fertility or the risk of miscarriage. You should be tested to determine whether you are immune to rubella, which can cause serious birth defects if a woman contracts it early in pregnancy—and if you are not, you can be immunized. Certain other blood tests may be advised if you are in a population group known to have a higher-than-average risk of particular inherited disorders, such as Tay-Sachs disease among Jews, or sickle-cell trait among blacks. And, not least, it's helpful to have an assessment of your state of health so that you can be sure your pregnancy will begin under the best possible conditions.

P.A.H.

# Part One

## The Countdown Begins

YOU'VE MISSED A PERIOD. MAYBE, JUST MAYBE, YOU'RE pregnant. How does your physician find out? How will you and your doctor determine the date your baby will arrive? What are the essential tests that must be performed, and the plans that must be made, just as soon as the fact of your pregnancy is established?

These first four chapters spell out detailed answers to those questions. For a first-time mother, they're required reading. If you're already a parent, you'll find some memory refreshers here—and perhaps some new-to-you wisdom as well.

# 1. Are You Really Pregnant?

"I wonder if I'm pregnant." Most women have probably asked themselves this question at one time or another, and many times a week I see patients who want me to confirm or deny the possibility of pregnancy.

Symptoms such as morning sickness or unusual tiredness may suggest pregnancy, and a physical examination can often confirm it—but not always. The early physical signs of pregnancy I look for in an examination, such as a bluish color of the vagina and cervix and a softening and enlarging of the uterus, do not appear until six to eight weeks after the last menstrual period. And if a woman is overweight or unable to relax during the pelvic exam, the size of her uterus may be difficult to evaluate.

If there is any doubt after the exam whether a woman is pregnant, I will usually perform a pregnancy test; it can be done in two minutes. I'll ask her for a urine sample, and by the time she is dressed, I'll know the result. If all my information—her symptoms, any signs I found when I examined her, and the pregnancy test—is consistent, I feel confident in answering her question "Am I pregnant?"

Pregnancy tests are not perfect, however, and it is important to understand how they work and why they are sometimes inaccurate. All pregnancy tests are based on the detection of *human chorionic gonadotrophin (HCG)*, a hormone that is normally produced only during pregnancy. Beginning very shortly after a fertilized egg implants within the uterus, HCG is produced by the placental tissues in increasing amounts; it reaches a peak concentration approximately 60 to 80 days after the onset of a woman's last menstrual period. HCG is excreted through the kidneys, and so it can be detected in the urine (it can also be measured in the blood).

During the 1940s and 1950s, when a woman thought she might be pregnant, a sample of her urine was injected into a test animal—a mouse, rat, rabbit, or frog. After a period of time, in some cases as long as five days, the animal would be killed and examined. Certain specific changes in its ovaries (or, in the case of the frog, sperm ejection) would indicate that there had been HCG in the urine and so confirm the pregnancy.

In the 1960s, pregnancy tests that could be done more quickly were developed. These "immunologic" tests, the type usually used today, employ antibodies to detect HCG in the urine. The test can be performed either on a glass slide, giving a result in about two minutes, or in a test tube, which requires about two hours. Some tests are more sensitive than others; that is, they can detect smaller amounts of HCG. Most are sensitive enough to detect the level of HCG present about one to two weeks after a missed menstrual period or about six weeks after the last period.

In the mid-1970s, various kits for home pregnancy testing became available. However, one early test had a 50 percent error rate—in other words, a woman could have made the diagnosis just as well by flipping a coin! This test has fortunately been withdrawn from the market. The ones currently available are more accurate and are very similar to those used in doctors' offices and labs. They are sensitive enough to detect pregnancy about two weeks after a missed period.

Home pregnancy tests clearly have the advantage of providing the privacy and anonymity important to many women. And since they can encourage women to recognize pregnancy early and to become involved in their own care, they can serve a useful purpose. Their main drawback, however, is that an incorrect result could cause a pregnant woman to delay visiting her doctor. Therefore, a woman should consult her doctor if she has symptoms of pregnancy, even if the test is negative.

Some women are now asking about the early diagnosis of pregnancy using very sensitive blood tests, called *radioimmunoassay* and *radioreceptor assay* tests, which can detect HCG very shortly after a pregnancy is established in the uterus; they may be positive even *before* the first missed menstrual period. Because these tests employ radioactive substances to detect HCG, they are available only at medical centers or through commercial laboratories. Compared with urine tests, they can be quite expensive, and they are often reserved for situations in which complications of pregnancy are suspected. Most women can wait the extra one or two weeks needed for the HCG to reach a level detectable by a urine test.

It must be stressed that both home tests and doctor's office or lab tests can give inaccurate results. A *false-negative* result of a urine test (indicating that a woman is not pregnant when, in fact, she is) is far more common than a *false-positive* one (indicating that a woman is pregnant when she isn't). Following are some factors that could cause an incorrect result:

- The most common reason for a false-negative result is that the test was performed too early in a pregnancy for the HCG to have risen to a detectable level. This is why a woman is usually asked for a "first morning" urine sample: the urine is more concentrated then and is thus more likely to give a positive result if she is pregnant.
- Conditions such as a threatened miscarriage or an ectopic pregnancy may cause a false-negative test result.
- HCG is similar in structure to *luteinizing hormone (LH)*, a hormone that stimulates the release of an egg from an ovary. A pregnancy test sensitive to very small amounts of HCG may react with LH instead, giving a false-positive result.
- Certain medical problems that may cause blood or protein to be present in the urine, such as an active bladder or kidney infection, can lead to inaccurate results. So can certain tumors that produce measurable amounts of HCG.
- Various medications, including some high-blood-pressure pills and some medicines used to treat psychiatric problems, can cause false-positive results.
- Mistakes in performing or reading the test may give an inaccurate result. The instructions for home pregnancy tests must be followed closely, but they are occasionally difficult to understand. The tests may be inaccurate if exposed to sun, detergent, temperature extremes, or shaking, or if read too soon or too late.

Because of these problems—some fairly common, some quite rare—I recommend that a physical examination be performed to confirm a pregnancy test result.

The following situation is not uncommon. Jane D. came to see me because she thought she might be pregnant. She and her husband have a three-year-old son and had been trying to conceive again. She told me that her periods had been very regular, coming every 28 days, but that her last period had begun 37 days before and that her breasts were tender. She had used a home pregnancy test kit, but it gave a negative result. When I examined her, I found that her uterus was of normal size, but I pointed out that it was really too soon for it to be enlarged. I discussed the most common reasons for a pregnancy test to be incorrect, and I suggested that she return in a week. I told her she probably was pregnant and that she should begin to care for herself as if she were. When she returned, the pregnancy test and the examination were positive, and I shared her delight as we began to discuss her prenatal care.

P.A.H.

# 2. When Is the Baby Due?

Janice was excited about her first pregnancy. She and her husband had been attempting to conceive for about a year. Since her last menstrual period had begun two months before, on April 10, she figured she was currently two months pregnant and calculated that the baby would arrive around January 17. After I examined her, we discussed the due date.

There were several questions in my mind that required clarification: Was her last menstrual period normal? Had it come on the expected day, with the usual amount of flow, and lasted the usual amount of time? Janice replied that it had been much lighter and had lasted only two days instead of the usual five or six. It had also started two days early, which had never happened before. Her last truly normal period had begun on March 10. Janice had also experienced mild nausea and breast tenderness since the first or second week in April and had performed a home pregnancy test that was positive on April 20.

At this point, the picture was clear; Janice's baby was due around December 17, not a month later as she had calculated. I explained that the size of the uterus indicated she was thirteen weeks pregnant instead of nine weeks. The bleeding Janice had experienced in April was not a normal period. The time the symptoms of pregnancy began and the fact that the home pregnancy test was positive in mid-April confirmed that the pregnancy was further advanced than Janice had thought.

"When is the baby due?" is the most frequently asked question at the first prenatal visit. The answer can usually be supplied readily, but many pieces of information from the patient's medical history and the physical examination are used to determine the due date. Since a due date is generally calculated from the last menstrual period (the first day, not the last day, of menstrual flow), I encourage all women to note the dates of their menstrual periods on a calendar. This information is not only helpful in calculating a due date, it is also useful for a woman in learning more about her individual cycle.

Many women who are attempting to conceive pay attention to symptoms experienced during ovulation to determine their fertile period. Symptoms may include breast tenderness, *mittelschmerz*—a twinge of pain or an achy sensation from the ovary on the left or right side—and an increase in vaginal discharge resulting from the effect of estrogen on cervical mucus, making it thin, watery, and more abundant.

In addition, some women plot their temperatures when they first awaken; the result is called a *basal body-temperature chart*. After ovulation, the level of progesterone increases. One of the effects of progesterone is to raise body temperature, so a temperature chart should indicate a sustained elevation after ovulation. This information can be most useful in helping to pinpoint the date of conception and in determining a due date.

The average duration of pregnancy is 280 days from the first day of the last menstrual period. Note that this number is not based on the date of conception. The average pregnancy lasts ten lunar months, or a little more than nine calendar months. But "four months pregnant" could mean sixteen weeks from the last menstrual period, sixteen weeks from conception, or 124 days (four months of 31 days each) from either the last menstrual period or the date of conception. The standard and more accurate way of referring to the duration of pregnancy is in terms of weeks from the beginning of the last menstrual period, with an average full-term pregnancy lasting 40 weeks.

The due date, or estimated date of confinement, can be derived from date of onset of the last menstrual period by using Nägele's rule, a formula devised by an early-nineteenth-century German obstetrician: Subtract three months from the date of the last menstrual period, then add seven days. If the last menstrual period began on June 10, for example, the due date would be March 17. The rule generally provides an accurate due date for women with regular cycles of the average length of 28 days. For women whose menstrual periods are irregular or for whom the normal cycle is longer than 28 days, it may be less reliable.

In using this method of establishing a due date, it is essential to determine when the last menstrual period actually occurred. I always ask my patients, as I did Janice, if the last period was a *normal* one, since it is not uncommon for a woman to have a small amount of bleeding or spotting in early pregnancy. Some women experience some bleeding when the embryo implants within the endometrial cavity at about the time of the next expected menstrual period or a little before. If it is interpreted as a normal period, the calculated due date may be off by a month.

The size of the uterus is also a factor in determining the due date. The uterus begins to increase noticeably in size at approximately six weeks from the last menstrual period. An examination during the first trimester (first thirteen weeks of pregnancy) can be very valuable in confirming a due date. As the pregnancy progresses, measurements of the size of the uterus continue to be important, but there is more individual variation among women. The uterus reaches the level of the woman's umbilicus (navel) at approximately twenty weeks. Thereafter, the height of the uterus, as measured from the top of the pubic bone to the top of the uterus, increases by approximately one centimeter per week up until the middle of the third trimester. Of course there is a reasonable amount of variation that may influence these measurements: A woman may be tall or short, thin or heavy, short-waisted or long-waisted; the bladder may be full or empty; and the baby may be in a transverse or oblique position. But in general, serial measurements of the fundal height (the *fundus* is the top part of the uterus) will allow an obstetrician to assess if there is a major deviation from the average range. If so, the due date may need to be confirmed by other means, such as an ultra-sound examination.

Because home pregnancy tests do not become positive until approximately six or seven weeks from the last menstrual period, knowing the date such a test was performed may provide additional information regarding the gestational age of the fetus.

*Quickening*, when the mother first perceives fetal move-ment, is another piece of information that can be helpful in dating a pregnancy. It usually occurs between sixteen and twenty weeks' gestation, although women may sometimes confuse these sensations with intestinal movement or abdom-inal muscle contractions.

The fetal heartbeat can first be heard with a fetal stetho-scope at approximately twenty weeks. This date, too, goes into the equation. (With a *Doppler*—ultrasound—instru-ment, the heartbeat can be heard earlier, at about ten weeks.)

Precise knowledge of the gestational age of the fetus may be critical in the management of obstetric complications. But aside from the medical importance, an expectant couple nat-urally want to know and plan for the birth date of their child. I try to give my patients the best estimate of a date of de-livery based on all the information that I have. It is, how-ever, important to understand that this date is only an estimate and certainly not a guarantee that the baby will be born on the given day. A couple can rest assured that two weeks earlier or later than the due date is well within normal limits.

P.A.H.

# 3. Blood Tests and Other Tests

Constance came to see me for her first prenatal visit. She was returning from the lab after having blood drawn for routine prenatal testing. "Those vampires!" she exclaimed. "What on earth do they want all that blood for?"

Like Constance, many women are surprised that so much blood is needed for testing. Although the amount of blood drawn might seem excessive, it is used for many tests for various purposes. Blood tests as well as urine tests have become an integral part of prenatal care and have been developed to detect and prevent potential problems. Here are the tests you can expect during your prenatal visits.

- *Complete blood count (CBC).* Blood hemoglobin and hematocrit are measured to determine if a woman is anemic. It is repeated during the third trimester of pregnancy.
- *Blood type.* A person's blood is generally one of four types: A, B, AB, or O. If a blood transfusion is required at any point during pregnancy or delivery, the blood to be transfused is always matched to the mother's blood, since some blood types are incompatible.
- *Rh factor.* Since the fetus inherits blood characteristics from both the mother and the father, the baby's blood type may differ from the mother's, and it may contain substances that are incompatible with the mother's blood. A problem can occur, for example, when the mother's blood is Rh negative and the fetus has inherited the Rh-positive factor from the father; this refers to certain blood markers, or antigens, which are present in Rh-positive

blood and are not found in blood that is Rh negative. If an Rh-negative mother becomes sensitized to the blood of her Rh-positive fetus, she may form antibodies that will destroy her fetus's blood cells, since they contain antigens not present in her own blood.

This sensitization rarely occurs during a first pregnancy, but it may happen at the time of delivery and can affect subsequent children. It can be prevented if an unsensitized Rh-negative mother whose child is Rh positive is given an injection of immune globulin within approximately 72 hours of delivery. Rh-negative women should also receive this injection if they have a miscarriage, ectopic pregnancy, or abortion, or undergo amniocentesis.

- *Antibody screen.* A mother may produce antibodies to other factors in her fetus's blood. Since some of these can cause a *hemolytic* (blood-destroying) disease of the fetus and newborn, a screening test is routinely performed to detect them.

- *Syphilis.* The detection of syphilis during pregnancy is especially critical. Not only must a mother and her sexual partner be treated to prevent complications for themselves, but it is particularly important that the mother be treated in order to prevent the multiple problems associated with congenital syphilis. The consequences for an infant with syphilis are so severe that syphilis screening is now legally required in most states. A positive result on an initial screening test is not proof that a woman has syphilis, but if further testing proves positive, she and her partner will be treated, usually with penicillin. Fortunately, syphilis is unable to cross the placenta into the fetus until the fifth month of pregnancy. This allows plenty of time to treat the mother early in pregnancy and to protect the baby.

- *Rubella.* Popularly known as German measles, rubella is a mild viral infectious disease that can cause serious congenital abnormalities in the child, such as heart malformations, deafness, and mental retardation, if the mother has the infection during pregnancy. A blood test will determine if a woman is immune to the disease. Immunity is acquired either by having had rubella or through vaccination. Women who are not immune should be vaccinated. The vaccine should not be given during pregnancy, however, because it is possible (though unlikely) for the vaccine to affect the fetus.

The symptoms of several illnesses may mimic rubella, and even though a woman may believe she has had the disease in the past, it is important to document whether she actually did have it. A test indicating immunity can be reassuring for a pregnant woman if there is any question that an illness during the pregnancy might actually be rubella.

- *Sickle-cell anemia screen.* Sickle-cell anemia is a serious disease affecting a small percentage of American blacks. Most people who have this form of anemia are aware of the disease, since it produces severe symptoms at an early age. Sickle-cell anemia is an unusual but serious problem during pregnancy.

  Approximately 8 to 10 percent of American blacks have the sickle-cell trait, which means that they have one sickle-cell gene but do not actually have the disease. Woman who have the sickle-cell trait have a tendency to develop bladder infections while pregnant but otherwise have no special problems with pregnancy. The partner of a woman who carries the sickle-cell trait should also be tested. If he carries the trait, their children have a 25 percent chance of having sickle-cell disease and a 50 percent chance of being carriers. Screening should be done early in the pregnancy, so that the couple can receive appropriate counseling about the risks of sickle-cell disease for their children.

- *Blood glucose.* Blood-sugar (glucose) measurements are recommended as screening tests for certain individuals. Women who have had a pregnancy loss, delivered a large infant, have a strong family history of diabetes, or show glucose in their urine are at risk of developing slightly elevated blood-sugar levels during pregnancy. This problem, which is sometimes called *gestational diabetes*, usually resolves after delivery, but women who develop it require special diets and close observation during the pregnancy to make sure their fetuses are growing properly.

One common screening test, generally done at about 28 weeks' gestation, entails drinking a concentrated sugar solution. The blood-glucose level is then checked an hour later. If the results of this screening test are abnormal, futher testing, usually a three-hour glucose-tolerance test, is performed before the diagnosis of gestational diabetes is made.

- *Urinalysis.* A microscopic and chemical analysis of a urine specimen is performed. The sample is checked for protein and glucose. The presence of bacteria and white blood cells may indicate a bladder infection. During pregnancy, such infections may be without symptoms, and if a bladder infection is left untreated, a more serious kidney infection may develop.
- *Pap smear.* If a Pap smear has not been performed recently, a scraping of the cervix will be taken and analyzed to detect any abnormal or precancerous cells. A young woman rarely has evidence of an actual cancer, but precancerous cells may be detected at a time when treatment can be easily instituted.
- *Other venereal diseases.* If a woman has had a sexually transmitted disease in the past, a cervical culture for gonorrhea may be performed so that she can be treated with antibiotics should the test prove positive. If she has a history of herpes infection, a cervical culture for herpes may also be taken.
- *Tuberculosis.* If a woman lives in an area where tuberculosis is still a problem, or if she has been exposed to the disease, she is likely to be given a skin test for TB.

Lab tests have become a routine part of prenatal care, and understanding their importance may help to ease the sting of the "vampire's bloodletting." These tests are invaluable for detecting and preventing potential problems and in helping physicians to provide the best possible care for both mother and child.

P.A.H.

# 4. Your Checkup Schedule

Even very secure people may feel pangs of anxiety in their doctor's office. Often it is not concern that the doctor will find an illness but rather the uncertainty of facing an unknown experience that gives the patient a sense of insecurity. Pregnant women sometimes experience these feelings too, even if they are well prepared for childbirth, so it is helpful to review what prenatal visits are for; by sharing this information we can reduce the fear of the unknown as much as possible.

There may be some differences from one obstetrician's or midwife's practice to another, and from one patient to another. Some tests may be done at different visits, and in specific instances additional tests may be indicated. But for the most part the basics are constant. I will review what happens in my office on a visit-by-visit basis.

Usually a newly pregnant woman comes to my office when her menstrual period is two weeks late and she wants confirmation of a fact that she is aware of, or at least suspects. By obstetrical definition, she is six weeks pregnant, with 34 weeks to complete before term.

If the patient is new, I start with a detailed medical history. We talk of operations, illnesses, medicines taken in the past, of drug reactions and allergies, of previous pregnancies and their outcome. I ask questions about the couple's families, their health and occupations, and about illnesses that run in the family. And I perform a pelvic examination to confirm the pregnancy, take a Papanicolaou smear for cancer detection, and examine the vagina for vaginitis or any other infection.

At this visit, as at each visit during pregnancy, I must correlate the size of the uterus with the duration of the pregnancy. The uterus may be disproportionately small, as in the case of an ectopic pregnancy, or if ovulation was late, or if the embryo is unhealthy and a miscarriage will soon occur. The uterus will be larger than expected if the pregnancy is further along than the mother realizes or if there is a multiple pregnancy.

I also check the pelvic measurements to see if labor will be easy, or perhaps difficult. One doesn't make a decision about a cesarean section at this time, however: Even a small pelvis can enlarge because of the relaxing effects of the pregnancy hormones on the pelvic ligaments as the pregnancy continues.

After the examination I tell my patient my findings in detail. We discuss diet, vitamins, activities, and any special instructions. If everything appears normal, we set the next appointment in one month.

During the second visit, usually a month after the first—that is, at ten weeks of pregnancy—I answer any questions that have occurred to my patient or her husband following the excitement of the first, confirmatory visit. We also discuss any complaints, such as nausea or tiredness, review diet, and outline future plans.

I do a general physical examination at this visit, not to try to find disease so much as to learn what is normal for a particular person. A general physical includes examining the mouth, eyes, glands of the neck, the heart, lungs, and the breasts; palpating the abdominal organs such as the liver and spleen; and taking the blood pressure. I do not do another pelvic exam at this point unless there is a specific indication for it.

I also double-check the duration and health of the pregnancy by palpating the growing uterus, which can now just be felt above the pubic bone. If there is any discrepancy between the duration of the pregnancy and the size of the uterus, a *sonogram*—a sound-wave picture—of the uterus is ordered. (I see no reason for routine sonography of all pregnant women. Special tests should be done only to provide necessary specific information, not to satisfy curiosity or merely because the machine is available.)

At either the second or the third prenatal visit I begin to do the tests that are a regular feature of prenatal care: urine tests to check for glucose and to evaluate kidney function (these are repeated at each succeeding visit), blood tests for syphilis and anemia, determination of the mother's blood type, Rh status, immunity to rubella, and so on.

I also measure the mother's blood pressure at each visit in order to see how efficiently her heart is meeting the increased circulatory and oxygen-transfer needs of pregnancy. When the pregnancy is difficult for the mother, her blood pressure will rise; that may signal a condition called toxemia, which must be treated promptly in order to protect both mother and baby.

From the fourteenth through the thirty-fourth week, visits continue on a routine monthly basis. This is the time when there is the least chance of complication for either the mother or the baby, and the visits are as brief or as lengthy as they need to be to answer any questions and to monitor the essentials of the pregnancy. I record weight gain and continue to test blood pressure and urine. I check how large the uterus is and feel the baby to measure its size and growth. These visits enable me to make sure that the mother is efficiently keeping up with the needs of the baby and that the baby is growing properly.

During the second trimester I also do a relatively new test— checking the alpha-fetoprotein level of the mother's blood. If this is elevated, it is a signal that there may be an abnormality in the development of the baby's nervous system. We also schedule any special tests that may be indicated, such as amniocentesis.

Sometime during this period, usually during the fifth month, the fetal heartbeat becomes audible, so I listen for it and check it at each visit.

During the last month of pregnancy, there is a new spirit to our visits, which occur weekly and sometimes more often. At each visit the question is either directly asked or implied: "When will the baby come?" We discuss how to recognize labor, what contractions feel like, and what to do when labor starts.

The special part of these visits is the pelvic examination, for this is what will predict the events of the coming few weeks. The exam enables me to feel the presenting part of the baby, and I feel the cervix to see if it is *effaced* (thinned out) and/

or dilated in order to determine whether labor may begin soon.

By the time my patient starts labor, I have examined her on about thirteen occasions. During these visits, we have learned to relax with each other and to communicate freely and honestly. Ideally, each visit is better than the previous one, and labor and delivery turn out to be the best encounter of all.

G.G.P.

# Part Two

ॐ

# Nine Months' Lifestyle

PREGNANCY ISN'T AN ILLNESS BUT A WHOLLY NATURAL CONdition. Most of your activities—at home, at work, at leisure—can and will continue unchanged. Yet, because there *is* another small being developing within your body, there *are* some special considerations.

Just as you are allotting time in your schedule to check in with your obstetrician or nurse-midwife once a month in order to be sure your pregnancy is proceeding as it should, you'll be conscious—in some cases, you *should* be conscious—of some other concerns, as well. Some represent necessary modifications in your lifestyle; others are simply factors of which it's wise to be aware. The next nine chapters offer guidance in these areas.

# 5. Nutrition Basics

"Eating for two" has been many a pregnant woman's excuse for overindulgence. While it is true that the growing fetus depends on its mother to meet nutritional needs, it is not true that these needs consist of double adult-size portions of chocolate cake and ice cream.

It is important that a pregnant woman eat a well-balanced diet, one that supplies enough energy and nutrients to satisfy her own needs as well as those of her unborn child. Pregnancy is not a time for weight reduction, nor is it a time for massive weight gain beyond what is necessary for appropriate growth of fetal and maternal tissues.

Both the nutritional status a woman has maintained prior to pregnancy and her diet during pregnancy are important for her and for her baby. A woman who is significantly underweight prior to pregnancy is more likely to have a low-birth-weight baby. A woman who is significantly overweight (more than 20 percent over the ideal weight for her height) prior to pregnancy is herself at some increased risk, primarily because of other medical problems associated with obesity, such as high blood pressure and diabetes.

To ensure good eating habits during your pregnancy, it's important to understand what comprises a well-balanced diet and what special dietary requirements pregnant women have. They fall in a number of nutritional areas.

- *Calories.* The calorie is a measure of energy. All foods provide energy as they are utilized by the body. Pregnancy increases the need for energy to create new fetal tissue, provide for higher maternal metabolism, and allow you to perform daily activities while carrying additional weight. It is relatively easy for most Americans to consume enough calories to meet their needs. Approximately 2,300 calories a day, or an increase of about 300 calories a day, are necessary for pregnancy.
- *Protein.* Pregnant women need more protein to provide for fetal and maternal tissue growth. Proteins are made

up of amino acids; some amino acids are essential—that is, they cannot be synthesized from other substances— and some are found only in animal proteins. (Vegetarian diets that contain no milk products or eggs are deficient in these essential amino acids.) The daily requirement for protein is approximately 45 grams per day for nonpregnant women and increases to 70 to 80 grams per day for women during pregnancy.

- *Folic acid.* An essential substance needed by cells that are dividing rapidly, folic acid can be found in foods such as liver, leafy green vegetables, and legumes. Some physicians advise routine supplementation of folic acid, while others recommend extra folic acid only for those women at risk for folate deficiency—women who have had multiple gestations, take anticonvulsants, have intestinal absorption problems, or have taken oral contraceptives prior to pregnancy.
- *Vitamins.* Vitamins are necessary for a wide variety of metabolic functions. They must be supplied in the diet, since they cannot be manufactured by the human body.

There are great differences of opinion regarding the optimal amounts of vitamins required for good health and whether or not dietary sources are adequate. Some physicians recommend prenatal vitamin supplements, while others do not. We may find someday that our current recommended daily allowances (RDA) of vitamins are insufficient, but until further research proves the point, the recommended daily allowance is our best guideline. There is no firm evidence to suggest that vitamins and minerals in amounts greater than the RDA are beneficial; in fact, excess consumption of some vitamins (A, D, and K, for example) can be harmful.

If a woman's diet during pregnancy is truly well balanced, vitamin supplements are probably unnecessary. It is important, however, to make sure your diet supplies the following vitamins:

*Vitamin A:* Sources include milk, butter, liver, and dark green and yellow vegetables. Vitamin A is fat-soluble and may accumulate in the liver.

*Vitamin D* is also a fat-soluble vitamin and is involved in calcium metabolism. A precursor of vitamin D can be manufactured by the body, but sunlight is required to produce the active form. Fortified foods such as milk, cheese, and yogurt supply the daily requirements for most women.

*Vitamin E* is contained in wheat germ, seed oils, cereals, egg yolks, nuts, and legumes. Relatively small increases in vitamin E are required in pregnancy, and supplementation is generally felt to be unnecessary.

*Vitamin K,* important in blood clotting, is synthesized by bacteria that normally reside in the intestines. Supplementation is not necessary. An injection of vitamin K is given to most newborns to prevent potential bleeding disorders.

The *B Vitamins* and *Vitamin C* are water soluble; they are excreted in the urine and cannot be stored, and deficiencies may result if the supply of these vitamins does not meet the demand. Sources of vitamin C include fruits, especially citrus, and some vegetables. Whole grains, leafy vegetables, liver, milk, and eggs contain B vitamins. Care should be taken in preparing foods, since these vitamins are often partially destroyed by cooking and refining.

• *Minerals*. These dietary substances are also necessary for a variety of metabolic functions. It is especially important for pregnant women to consume an adequate supply of the following.

*Iron:* The requirement for iron rises during pregnancy to allow for an increase in the number of maternal blood cells. In addition, the fetus needs iron and will draw iron from the mother, whether or not she has any to spare. Most healthy women do not have sufficient iron reserves and do not absorb enough iron to provide for the needs of pregnancy. Supplements are therefore recommended to prevent iron deficiency, although attention to foods rich in iron—lean meats, liver, and dark leafy vegetables—is still important.

*Calcium:* A mineral necessary for fetal bone formation, calcium is found primarily in dairy products. The recommended daily allowance for calcium can be met by drinking approximately four eight-ounce glasses of milk per day or by substituting cheese, yogurt, or ice cream for some of the milk. Some women, however, cannot tolerate milk products without experiencing intestinal disturbances. For these women, calcium supplements are necessary.

*Other Minerals:* Zinc, copper, magnesium, and manganese are necessary in pregnancy and are supplied by fish, meats, eggs, dried beans, milk, fruits, and vegetables.

• *Fiber:* Dietary fiber is not absorbed by the body; it aids digestion and helps to prevent constipation by adding bulk to the stools and drawing water into the intestines. Since constipation is a common problem during pregnancy, a diet rich in whole-grain breads and cereals with bran is recommended.

Pregnancy is a good time to learn about nutrition and the benefits of a healthful diet. A baby-to-be provides many women with added incentive to eat well-balanced meals. After the baby is born, good eating habits can be easily continued, and the nutritional principles learned during pregnancy can be incorporated into the lifestyle of the entire family.

P.A.H.

# 6. How Much Weight Gain?

All pregnant women are concerned about their weight changes, and yet the subject is not that complicated.

The special features of pregnancy entail about 21 pounds: the fetus, about seven pounds; amniotic fluid, about two pounds; the placenta, about one pound; the uterus, about two and one-half pounds; increase in the mother's blood volume, about four pounds; increase in breast size, about two and one-half pounds; and general fluid retention, about two pounds. This doesn't mean that you *must* gain 21 pounds during pregnancy. If you gain less, your body itself will give up some weight, and you will actually be lighter after you give birth than you were before becoming pregnant. If you gain more, you will be heavier than you were when you started. A pregnant woman of ideal body weight requires an extra 300 calories a day for fetal- and pregnancy-related growth to occur without fat loss in the mother.

Concern about excessive maternal weight gain, which has preoccupied gynecologists and prospective mothers, has been matched in recent years by concern with maternal undernutrition.

In 1976, researchers in India reported their findings on maternal undernutrition in the *American Journal of Obstetrics and Gynecology*. They studied three groups of mothers, with average caloric intakes of 2,900, 2,400, and 1,600 calories per day; the average protein intakes for these mothers were 76, 67, and 52 grams per day, respectively. The infants of mothers in the lower groups were substantially smaller, and the placentas were also significantly smaller.

Newspapers reported these findings in frightening ways— an example of exploitative journalism that manipulates mothers' honest concern about their unborn babies' health in order to sell newspapers. In fact, the findings in India represent the physiology of women who are chronically protein deficient because of a lifetime of poor nutrition. They do not apply to healthy women who are well nourished.

The recommended protein intake for nonpregnant women is one gram per kilogram of body weight per day. For the American woman of average weight, this means about 60 grams of protein per day. During pregnancy, a large amount of protein-based tissue is formed every day. This is the muscle and tissue of the fetus, the enlarging placenta, the increase in the size of the muscular uterus, and the increase in the mother's blood volume—all the factors responsible for the weight gain mentioned earlier.

Because of these factors, the intake of protein should be raised by 20 to 30 grams per day. While none of the Indian women studied (even those with normal infants) consumed this much protein, most American women take in more, even when they are not pregnant. To give you an idea of how little this is for Americans, remember that two hamburgers more than supply this amount of protein. A quart of milk, regular or skim, has 32 grams of protein.

I tell my patients that weight is purely a cosmetic issue during pregnancy. If you like your weight the way it is, then gain just about twenty pounds, since that's all you're going to lose when you give birth.

G.G.P.

# 7. Morning Sickness (Maybe)

It seems unfair that the happy early weeks of pregnancy are often marred by sickness. Yet almost 50 percent of pregnant women suffer from nausea or vomiting during the first trimester, usually first thing in the morning. This "morning sickness" is such an unpleasant sensation, and is so distinctive, that once a pregnant woman has experienced it, she can always distinguish it from every other sickness. Many women can announce to their doctors, "I'm sure I'm pregnant; I just feel that sickness. When do you want to examine me?" Sometimes nausea occurs so soon after conception that it suggests pregnancy even before the menstrual period is missed.

Almost everyone has experienced nausea at one time or another. Usually, we quickly learn what stimuli make us nauseated and try to avoid them. But when a pregnant woman suffers from morning sickness, she is often at a loss for what to do.

A pregnant patient's nausea can also be frustrating to her doctor, who wants to help but who also wishes to avoid the use of drugs during pregnancy whenever possible. Most of the drugs that can stop nausea and vomiting have not been proved safe for use in early pregnancy. The doctor generally attempts to reassure the patient by reminding her that the nausea and vomiting usually pass by the twelfth week of pregnancy.

This observation about the self-limited aspect of the problem is true, but what is to be done in the meantime? Reviewing the physiology involved will help us to understand what positive measures can be undertaken to provide some relief.

Neurological studies have shown that there is a nausea and vomiting center located in the *medulla oblongata*—the brain stem, or portion of the brain joining the spinal cord to the upper brain. This vomiting center receives stimuli from different parts of the body and coordinates and controls them. The stimuli may result in nausea or, when they are strong enough, in vomiting.

Although we often blame the stomach for an attack of nausea or vomiting, it actually plays a passive role when vomiting occurs. The *pylorus*, the exit valve of the stomach, closes, and the stomach contents are expelled up the esophagus and through the mouth by spasmodic contractions of the abdominal muscles.

The stimuli that affect the vomiting center are varied. Often they are physical. An irritant in the stomach, such as bad food or excess acid, can lead to nausea or vomiting. So can a painful blow. Another example of a physical stimulus, though a far more subtle one, is the stretching of the uterine wall during pregnancy.

Some people may be affected by psychic, emotional or visual stimuli, such as unpleasant thoughts or sights.

Most of the vomiting stimuli in early pregnancy are probably related to changing levels of hormones in a pregnant woman's body, but there is still much uncertainty about which hormones are responsible and how they work.

Many researchers attribute nausea and vomiting to the high levels of the hormone called *human chorionic gonadotrophin* (HCG), present during the first trimester of pregnancy, when morning sickness is most common. HCG probably ensures that the ovaries continue to produce *progesterone*—necessary to maintain the uterine lining—until the placenta is producing enough. HCG is at its highest level about 70 days after conception, then gradually declines, reaching a stable lower level between 100 and 130 days after conception—about the time nausea and vomiting usually subside.

Other theories connect morning sickness with the increasing production of progesterone and estrogen, which may cause gastrointestinal disturbances, or to the change from ovarian to placental production of these hormones, a change that occurs during the second and third months after conception.

Moreover, because progesterone acts as a muscle relaxant, *peristalsis* (the contractions that move the intestinal contents) may be slowed, stomach emptying may be delayed, the stomach may dilate, and stomach acid may build up to irritating amounts.

Progesterone also helps the uterine wall to expand, and this stretching may further stimulate the vomiting center in the brain. Often, nausea is worse if a woman is bearing twins; this may be related to increased muscle stretching and to the high levels of HCG found during multiple pregnancies.

The tiredness and lack of energy common in early pregnancy—perhaps also due in part to hormonal changes—may make the vomiting center in the brain more sensitive to these and other stimuli, such as particular odors or flavors.

On the basis of these theories, we can formulate several self-help techniques to alleviate the nausea and vomiting of early pregnancy. Here are some suggestions:

- Reduce the sensitivity of the emetic center in the brain by sleeping more during early pregnancy. If you suffer from nausea or vomiting, try adding two to four extra hours of sleep a night, if possible.
- Try to neutralize or absorb irritating stomach acids. You may get a great deal of relief by eating small amounts often. It may help to eat or drink something even before getting out of bed in the morning. Carry dry crackers with you during the day and munch them whenever you feel you are becoming nauseated.

  Your doctor may also advise you to try one of the readily available antacids (you should not do so without such advice). It is probably wise not to use one that contains sodium bicarbonate, however, because high levels of sodium may build up in your body and cause excessive fluid retention.

- Avoid contributing to stomach fullness. Eat only small amounts at one time, so that you don't dilate your stomach.
- Vitamin $B_6$ (pyridoxine) is a preparation that may give you some relief from nausea or vomiting. Your doctor may recommend that you can safely take 50 milligrams twice a day. If you are suffering from severe nausea or vomiting, it may be advised that vitamin $B_6$ be given by injection until the condition improves. Vitamin $B_6$ may improve muscle tone, helping stomach emptying and peristalsis.
- If you discover that particular stimuli—certain smells, for example—cause an attack of nausea, try to avoid them whenever possible.

Vomiting that is so severe or prolonged that it leads to dehydration or compromises the nutritional needs of the mother or fetus is a serious cause for concern and should be treated by a doctor. Sometimes, though rarely, hospitalization may be necessary to ensure that proper fluid and mineral balances are maintained. *Mild* morning sickness, however, is a condition that, more than many others, may best be relieved by the pregnant woman herself.

G.G.P.

# 8. Cosmetic Concerns

Diane, pregnant with her first child, cornered her favorite source of medical information, Joan, one afternoon over a glass of iced tea. "I feel like a blimp," she confided tearfully. "I have stretch marks on my stomach, my ankles are swollen, and I have dark spots all over my face!" Joan empathized, since she had had three children herself: "I know it can seem that way at times. Have you asked your doctor about any of your concerns?" Diane conceded, "She's so busy, I don't want to bother her with these problems." Joan wisely suggested that she give it a try anyway: "Maybe she can explain what causes these things. Besides, when you smile, you look healthy and radiantly pregnant. No one else notices these things as much as you do."

Diane's concerns are very common, but the questions often don't get asked. Granted, physicians don't consider these to be major problems, and some doctors may not take the time to explain to their patients what happens to a woman's body during pregnancy. It is true that for the most part these problems are self-limited, but it is easier for a woman to deal with these changes if she anticipates them and understands why they occur.

Some of the first physical symptoms that may signal pregnancy are changes in the breasts. Many women feel a tingling sensation in the nipples, and their breasts feel full and tender. As the breasts increase in size, delicate veins beneath the skin become more visible, and the areas around the nipples, the areolae, become larger and darker in color. These changes occur because of increases in breast tissue, fluid, and fat in response to elevated hormone levels.

Our culture emphasizes the desirability of large breasts, leaving many small-breasted women feeling "underendowed," but the increase in breast size with pregnancy may lead these women to feel particularly attractive and sexy. If pregnancy and its physical changes are initially experienced as positive, a woman's self-image will benefit, too.

As pregnancy progresses, it is inevitable that a woman's

figure will change. At first, there is a thickening around the middle and only the hint of a protruding belly. Many women feel so proud to be pregnant that they announce it to the world by wearing maternity clothes very early in pregnancy. Others feel comfortable wearing regular clothing until the twentieth week or so. Every woman is an individual, and her body changes at its own individual pace. It's medically important only that clothes not bind or constrict.

Friends, relatives, and neighbors will certainly comment on a pregnant woman's changing proportions. Comments like, "My, you look so big; maybe it's twins," or "Are you sure you're due in July? You don't look that pregnant," can cause a woman to wonder if her baby is growing normally. These feelings should not be ignored. If something is bothering you, ask your doctor, but once you have asked and received a satisfactory answer—"The baby is growing normally," or "I don't think it's twins," or "The due date *is* most probably mid-July"—then forget and ignore the comments of others.

Weight and figure changes frequently cause stretch marks. Ninety percent of pregnant women have them, and they often "run in families." These pink or reddish, slightly depressed streaks commonly appear on the breasts and abdomen and sometimes on the thighs.

Although many special lotions and creams are marketed specifically for these marks, they are probably no more effective than any lubricating hand or body lotion; they make dry skin more pliable and soft, but they will not prevent stretch marks, nor will they cause them to fade. The best remedy for stretch marks is "tincture of time." The red or pink color fades to silver white, and the marks become thinner after delivery.

Many women complain of swollen ankles, feet, and legs, and even swollen fingers, especially during the third trimester (the last twelve to thirteen weeks) of pregnancy. This fluid retention and swelling, medically termed *edema*, is often a harmless side effect of pregnancy, but it can also signal preeclampsia or toxemia during the final trimester. These are serious complications; edema is accompanied by a rise in blood pressure, and protein can be detected in the urine. This is why urine checks for protein, blood-pressure monitoring, and questions about ankle swelling are routine components of prenatal visits in late pregnancy.

Simple edema may be uncomfortable, but it is not a serious cause for concern. It is best treated by bed rest; it often subsides during the night when a woman is lying down but worsens again during the day. Women who are bothered by swollen ankles should elevate their legs as frequently as possible and wear comfortable shoes or slippers, or even go barefoot in the summer. Support stockings may also help somewhat. Fortunately, the condition is usually short lived, since edema subsides quickly after the baby is born.

During pregnancy, there is an increase in skin pigmentation. In many women, the midline of the abdominal skin turns dark brown, forming what is called the *linea nigra*, or dark line. A similar cosmetic problem that occurs more frequently in brown-eyed, dark-haired women is the "mask of pregnancy," in which tan to dark brown patches appear over the forehead, nose, and cheeks. The increased pigmentation is a result of stimulation by the pregnancy hormones. Attempts at skin bleaching are not effective, although the use of a sunscreen containing PABA on the face during times of sun exposure may help to prevent further darkening. Again, these changes usually reverse themselves after delivery.

Some women also notice other types of skin changes during pregnancy. Dry skin is a common complaint. Sometimes tiny red spots appear on the trunk, chest, and back, and the palms of the hands turn markedly red. "Vascular spiders," minute red elevations of the skin resembling spiders in shape, frequently appear on the face, chest, and arms. None of these changes poses a medical problem, but they may cause needless worry if a woman isn't aware that they are common phenomena and not reasons for concern.

Several months after delivery, many women worry that they are losing their hair. Pregnancy does indeed affect the hair's growth cycle. In a nonpregnant woman, approximately 80 percent of the hairs on her head are in an active growth phase; the remainder are in a resting phase and eventually fall out. During pregnancy, fewer hairs are in the resting phase and more are growing. Since fewer hairs are being shed, hair may actually seem to be growing faster or becoming thicker.

After delivery, however, the growth phases revert to normal, and more hair falls out. This hair loss is seldom a significant problem, and if a woman does feel that her hair has grown thinner after her baby is born, she can be reassured that the prospects for normal hair regrowth are excellent.

It is easier for a woman to accept changes in her body during pregnancy when she is prepared for them and understands why they occur. They are just one aspect of being pregnant and should not become a major focus of concern. Most of these problems disappear after the baby is born anyway. If a pregnant woman sees herself as physically attractive in spite of these minor problems, she will feel better about herself and appear attractive to others, too.

P.A.H.

# 9. Sports and Exercise

From early on, pregnant women begin to wonder about how they are affecting the health and welfare of their new precious cargo. Women who are normally active in sports and athletics wonder if they may continue their activities, and women who are normally very sedentary begin to think about whether or not they should start an exercise program. Will exercise help or hurt the baby? Will exercise make labor easier? Are there any restrictions?

We can develop some sensible guidelines by considering the experiences of some actual women.

One of my patients, Mary W., is a serious jogger who had been jogging for many years before she became pregnant. She described her experiences to me: "I was running through my eighth month. Toward the end, I had to slow up, because I was getting stitches in my side. That was the only reason I got slower. I didn't feel any pressure in my vagina or from my uterus.

"I tried substituting exercises at home, you know, straight

leg lifts. But it wasn't the same. I missed my daily routine. So I got suited up in my sweats and I went back to the park with my running companion. While she would run the four-mile loop, I would slowly jog a one-mile loop, and we would then meet and walk home together. I had a lot of fun watching people's expressions when they noticed my big belly."

Scientists have studied the effects of a strenuous jogging program on a pregnant woman up to the time of delivery. One such study, conducted at the department of physiology at the University of Hawaii School of Medicine in Honolulu, found that there were no disturbances to the mother or to the fetus when a jogger's heart rate reached as high as 95 percent of her maximum when she was not pregnant.

Exercise has also been studied in animals; pregnant sheep are exercised on a treadmill, and the uterine blood flow and fetal oxygen levels are studied. It is known that blood flows from the pregnant uterus to the working muscle during periods of activity, and such studies of animals have shown that while exercise does not adversely affect normal fetuses, it often affects compromised fetuses.

This provides us with a primary principle: You should not do any exercise if you are having vaginal bleeding or if there is any other sign of fetal compromise during pregnancy. And to be perfectly safe, you should not exercise to maximum effort during pregnancy, because of the diversion of blood from the uterus to the working muscle. A good rule of thumb is that a pregnant woman who jogs or engages in any other strenuous exercise should be able to *talk* while exercising. If she can't converse while in motion, she's not getting enough oxygen— and should slow down.

When Mary W. experienced "stitches," she was suffering muscle spasms due to inadequate blood flow. She wisely responded to the signal and reduced her exertion. This emphasizes a second basic principle: Pain due to exercise in pregnancy is a signal to rest and to reevaluate the activity.

Linda B., another of my patients, is in the eighth month of her first pregnancy. An experienced and avid horsewoman, Linda still rides two hours every day.

She explains, "The only difference pregnancy makes now

is that when I dismount, my groin muscles hurt for five minutes. But then it stops and it doesn't hurt anymore. For the first few months there was no difference in my riding. But by the time I was four months pregnant I couldn't get my balance. Then by the next month, there was no problem. My main concern is the birth itself—and will I be unable to get back to riding quickly?"

As pregnancy progresses, the mother's center of gravity shifts forward and there is a compensating curvature of the lower back. This curvature is called *lumbar lordosis*. It causes a strain on posture, which Linda noticed at the end of her fourth month of pregnancy. By the next month, however, she had adapted to the changes in her body.

Skiers find that this shift forward in the center of gravity helps them to lean into the skis properly, as a good skier does. For this reason, I encourage my patients who are skilled and safety-concious skiers to continue the sport when they are pregnant. (Skiing at heights above 10,000 feet should be avoided, however, because of decreased oxygen, which may be harmful to the fetus.)

But the shifting center of gravity in pregnancy, and the resultant changes in posture and balance, provide a third basic principle: Pregnancy is *not* the time to start a *new* sport.

As far as Linda's concern about delivery: Dr. E. Zaharieva studied the effects of Olympic Games participation, both on women who had competed before pregnancy and childbirth and on women who competed after childbirth. The study was reported in the *Journal of the American Medical Association*.

There were no harmful effects. In fact, the second stage of labor, the stage of pushing and expelling the baby, was easier and shorter for athletes than for nonathletes. Furthermore, labor and delivery had no adverse effect on the athletes' future training and subsequent participation in the Games. I'm sure that Linda won't have to wait too long to get back to riding.

If pregnancy is not a time for starting a new sport, but you feel you should exercise, what can you do? Megan S., who is seven months pregnant, told me her experiences during her monthly visit: "I haven't exercised or done athletics since I've grown up. I started to feel aches in my thighs and groin—I thought that I had better get into shape. I sat on the floor and did arm and leg stretching. Then I would lie down and do leg lifts. The aches stopped after a few days, and I have continued my exercise every day since then. I'm in better shape now than when I started my pregnancy."

By lying on her back, Megan compensates for her lumbar lordosis. She uses her leg and arm muscles to work against the natural force of gravity. She does not subject her body to extremes of force or motion.

My own favorite exercise is walking and, like swimming, it is one of the best exercises of all for pregnant women. This is what Dr. Prudence B. Saur wrote about walking and exercise in pregnancy:

> Walking—I mean a walk, not a stroll—is a glorious exercise; it expands the chest and throws back the shoulders; it strengthens the muscles . . . it clears the complexion, giving roses to the cheeks and brilliancy to the eye. . . .
>
> Let a delicate lady *learn* to take exercise as a young child would *learn* to walk—by degrees; let her creep, and then go; let her gradually increase her exercise, and let her do nothing either rashly or inadvisedly. . . .

Dr. Saur presented her advice in *Maternity: A Book for Every Wife and Mother*, which was published in 1889, almost one hundred years ago.

G.G.P.

# 10. Travel Tips

It is the lucky pregnant woman who can break up the long nine months with travel and vacations, but invariably, she will have some apprehensions: Is it safe to fly? Can she take a long car ride? Generally, the normal pregnant woman can travel during her entire pregnancy until the time she is likely to go into labor, provided there is no danger that the trip itself might initiate labor.

The best guideline for air travel during pregnancy is the cervix. As long as the cervix (mouth of the uterus) is closed, most travel is safe. In the normal pregnant woman, the cervix stays closed at least through the seventh month. After that, you should have a pelvic examination before any substantial trip. If the cervix is found to be *effaced* (thinned out, less strong) or *dilated* (starting to open), there is a very definite risk of premature labor. And any woman with a history of premature labor must have a pelvic examination before *any* plane trip, at *any* time during pregnancy.

The pressurization of commercial airplanes becomes constant only upon reaching 8,000 feet. Consequently, at takeoff, there is an outward force of the amniotic fluid against the membranes, against the cervix. If the cervix is partially dilated, the membranes will bulge out and can rupture, causing premature birth. Upon landing, the membranes bulge in, with the same risk of rupture of membranes.

You can see, then, how the state of the cervix individualizes the advice. While a woman who is eight months pregnant with a slightly dilated cervix should not fly, a nine-months-pregnant woman with a tightly closed cervix may do so safely.

Airplane travel also presents the paradox of fluid retention and dehydration. Because of the pressures involved, most people get slightly *edematous* (retain fluid) on the plane. For that reason, I advise my patients to wear support hose on the plane. Plane food is usually very salty, further contributing to edema. It may therefore be a good idea to pack your own, nonsalty food. On the other hand, because of the dry, air-conditioned air, one tends to get dehydrated. You should drink ordinary water both before boarding and on a regular basis during a long flight.

Private-plane travel must be approached especially cautiously, since there are special risks to the fetus. In a pressurized commercial-airliner cabin, the fetus is obtaining sufficient oxygen to meet its needs. In a nonpressurized small plane, however, the oxygen content of the air decreases at higher altitudes, and the fetus can suffer oxygen deprivation. In order to protect the baby, you should not fly above 10,000 feet in a nonpressurized plane without breathing oxygen.

There is one risk factor shared by plane travel and car travel. Sitting for a long period of time tends to slow the return of blood from the legs. The circulation is slowed, and there is an increased risk of *thrombophlebitis*, or blood clots, usually in the lower legs. Pregnancy itself, due to hormones and the pressure of the enlarging uterus, also slows the return of blood from the legs. Therefore, the combination of pregnancy and the long ride is particularly dangerous.

For that reason, on an airliner, you should get up from your seat every hour and walk up and down the aisle. Similarly, during a long car ride, you should stop the car once every hour, get out, and stretch your legs; walking once around the car will suffice. You should not wear restrictive clothing, and the seat belt should not be too tight.

Travel by ship does not, of course, carry the risk of rarefied air. And strolling on the deck is an excellent way to recirculate the blood through your legs. But a pregnant woman is more susceptible to seasickness. If you have your doctor's permission, you can take an over-the-counter antinauseant after the twelfth week of pregnancy; prior to that time, you should obtain a prescription for a safe antinausea medicine from your doctor.

Although these are general prudent precautions, you should discuss your travel plans with your obstetrician, who will be able to add the specifics that apply to you in particular.

G.G.P.

# 11. The Question of Sex

Although the topic of sex and sexuality during pregnancy is no longer taboo, many women feel reluctant to ask their doctors about it. Nor is it a subject that physicians often bring up spontaneously. And despite the fact that sex during pregnancy is indeed a concern of many women, a lot of questions remain unanswered.

In addressing the issue, it is important to understand that there are many physical and emotional changes a woman and her partner must deal with. Sharing these experiences may bring a couple closer together, but their sexual relationship can also be stressed by them. And problems can be compounded by the fact that much misinformation has been disseminated through old wives' tales and outdated medical advice.

Traditionally, physicians have advised that intercourse be avoided during the last month or six weeks of pregnancy and during the six weeks after the baby is born, but these recommendations are based on little factual information. The medical literature itself also contains conflicting reports. During an uncomplicated pregnancy, however, sex is not harmful.

Some generalizations about sexual responses and changes during pregnancy can be made, but it is important to keep in mind that the responses of individual women or couples may be quite different from the average and still be normal.

With the confirmation of a planned pregnancy, many couples feel relieved; being pregnant means not having to worry about becoming pregnant. Some women even report an increase in desire or enjoyment of sex during this time.

However, the physical sensations that accompany the first trimester of pregnancy may decrease sexual desire. It's hard to feel sexy when you feel nauseated. It's important for the woman and her partner to discuss this, and for her partner to make an effort to understand that this is not a total rejection. Many women enjoy simply being held, cuddled, and caressed at this time. Communicating this is important, too, as one's partner may not be able to get the message if it is not explicitly stated.

The first trimester may also bring an increased need for sleep or rest. Many women say that they want nothing more in the evenings than to go to bed—to sleep—at eight o'clock! It helps to remember that nausea and fatigue generally diminish with the second trimester.

Another physical change that can affect lovemaking in early pregnancy is breast sensitivity. Tenderness and some pain are common, and avoidance of breast or nipple stimulation may be temporarily necessary. As the body adjusts to these changes, the tenderness usually resolves.

One fear some women or couples experience during the first trimester is that intercourse will cause a miscarriage. There is no medical evidence that this is true for normal pregnancies, but a physician may advise a woman who has had a miscarriage to avoid sex. If a woman has had spotting during early pregnancy or has had a previous miscarriage, she should ask her doctor whether intercourse should be avoided and, if so, for what period of time. Sometimes spotting results from a cervical irritation, and intercourse can aggravate the condition.

Remember, though, even if intercourse should be avoided during certain times, there are mutually enjoyable alternatives in lovemaking. Touching, massage, and other nongenital activities may be explored, as well as mutual masturbation or oral-genital sex. In fact, pregnancy may actually be a time when couples learn to enhance their sexual pleasure in a variety of ways. One activity that should be avoided during pregnancy, though, because it may cause severe or even fatal complications, is the practice of blowing or forcing air into the vagina.

Many women report that the second trimester is the most comfortable part of pregnancy. The nausea and fatigue of the first three months are gone, and the abdomen has not become large enough to interfere with comfort and easy movement. The fear of miscarriage has passed.

However, the baby is beginning to announce its presence

through the mother's enlarging abdomen, and the couple begin to contend with the realities of changing body size and shape. Other physical changes may include an increased amount of vaginal lubrication and vaginal engorgement or swelling. Partners may also begin to have some concerns about hurting the woman or baby during intercourse. It is important to remember, though, that intercourse will not harm the baby; it is well protected within the amniotic sac, and the cervix remains closed during this part of pregnancy.

Most physicians agree that in the absence of such complications as bleeding, ruptured membranes, cervical weakness (*incompetent cervix*), or threatened premature labor, there is no reason that couples should not continue to pursue normal sexual activity throughout pregnancy. It might be helpful to note that it is relatively common for orgasm to cause some mild uterine contractions. For most women, though, the evidence suggests that these are harmless and will not hurt the baby.

As the pregnancy progresses through the last trimester, however, the pregnant woman may experience such physical discomfort as indigestion, backache, and bloating, and she may not be feeling particularly attractive. She may need some extra reassurances—both verbal and physical—of her husband's continued love and support.

Labor and delivery, particularly when a husband is present, can be the ultimate experience of togetherness and love. But this emotional high point can also be accompanied by other feelings of fear and amazement, as the birth process involves an incredible stretch of the vagina. The father may well wonder if his wife's genital organs will ever be the same. Remarkably, the uterus and vagina do return to normal size.

The postpartum period also brings many physical changes, including the healing of the vaginal opening or episiotomy site (see chapter 41). People heal at different rates, but many women, even those who have had episiotomies, find that intercourse is possible after two or three weeks. Many doctors advise their patients to wait until the *lochia* (the normal vaginal discharge that follows childbirth) becomes scant and yellowish and the area is no longer tender, before having intercourse.

For most women, a six-week waiting period is probably not necessary. However, many factors in the postpartum period, including fatigue from full-time parenting, lack of sleep, or physical discomfort may influence sexual relations.

Breast-feeding can also have an effect. The hormonal changes result in decreased vaginal lubrication, and breasts may be tender. Milk may leak or spurt from the breasts during love-making. Most couples deal with these changes through open communication and good humor, but it does help to have some idea of what to expect.

Many couples approach the first time they have sex after the baby's birth with some apprehension; they may wonder if their sexual relationship will be the same. Often they discover, though, that their relationship has actually improved after the shared experiences of pregnancy and birth. There may be some vaginal pain, so a lubricant might be helpful. And especially during this time, gentleness and good communication are important in building a deep and trusting relationship.

P.A.H.

# 12. Smoking and Drinking

Picture for a moment a tiny baby, an unborn child, with a cigarette in her mouth. A frightful image, indeed. But when a pregnant woman lights up a cigarette, she is smoking for two. In spite of the fact that smoking has been linked to such chronic lung ailments as emphysema, bronchitis, and a variety of cancers, as well as to heart disease, many people choose to smoke. Often, these are conditions that develop later in life. For a pregnant woman, though, the effects of cigarette smoking are significant and immediate.

Studies have demonstrated that nicotine, a toxic substance contained in cigarette smoke, crosses the placenta and can affect the fetus by increasing the fetal heart rate. The placentas of smokers are also directly affected: Nicotine constricts placental blood vessels, which reduces the supply of oxygen. In addition, carbon monoxide inhaled in cigarette smoke reduces the capacity of the blood to carry oxygen. Oxygen provided by the mother's blood is essential for the healthy development and growth of the fetus. Although a number of questions remain about the effects of maternal smoking on fetal development, there are some particular problems that are known to occur among babies born to mothers who smoke.

It was first reported in 1957 that babies born to women who smoke during pregnancy are on average 200 grams (approximately seven ounces) lighter than babies born to women who do not smoke. Since then these findings have been confirmed by other studies. These babies do not reach their full growth potential prior to birth; they are undernourished even before they are born. And smokers' babies are likely to be shorter as well as lighter. It is important to note, however, that if a woman quits smoking during early pregnancy, her chances of having a low-birth-weight baby are similar to those of nonsmoking women.

Women who smoke are also more likely than nonsmokers to suffer miscarriages in early pregnancy. Smokers also have a higher risk of developing bleeding problems associated with early separation of the placenta (*placental abruption*) and abnormal implantation of the placenta (*placenta previa*). Both of these complications carry an increased risk of fetal death, and the more a woman smokes, the greater her chances of developing them. The early death rate is also higher for babies of smokers. In studies of victims of sudden infant death syndrome (SIDS), more of the mothers were found to be smokers than in a comparable control group.

Research suggests, too, that mothers' smoking may affect children's future growth, mental development, and behavior. Studies of children up to age seven have indicated that the children of smokers remain smaller—both shorter and lighter— than those of nonsmokers. The British Perinatal Mortality Survey, for example, included approximately 17,000 infants. When these children were traced and studied again at ages seven and eleven, both mental and physical growth were found to be slower in the children of smokers.

Once a woman understands the risks of smoking during pregnancy, it will be easier to decide to stop. It is certainly not easy for a person who habitually smokes cigarettes to give them up. The National Cancer Institute publishes a kit of booklets and posters, "Quit for Good," which is available to physicians for their patients' use. It contains a collection of tips that might prove useful in helping people to stop smoking.

Your partner can offer additional support for your decision to quit; the health and well-being of his wife and child is his concern, too. If he is a smoker, perhaps he can also make an effort to stop smoking. If he is not, his positive reinforcement for you when you don't smoke is more helpful than nagging or berating you when you do. It is also helpful for you and your partner to become more health conscious. By focusing on getting enough rest and exercise, eating nourishing foods, and planning healthful activities, you will feel better and so will your family.

If you feel that you cannot quit on your own, the American Cancer Society, the American Heart Association, the American Lung Association, and various other groups offer formal programs for people who smoke. Information about the risks of smoking and tips on quitting are available from these organizations and through your doctor's office.

If you are successful in giving up smoking during pregnancy, you demonstrate to yourself that you can kick the habit. Although the baby's health offers additional motivation, do not let yourself start smoking again after the baby is born. Children whose parents smoke are more likely to have frequent colds and respiratory infections. Besides, it is far easier to stay away from cigarettes than it is to go through the process of quitting again.

Ask your obstetrician for advice and help. It has been estimated that between one-quarter and one-third of all pregnant smokers quit, and another third cut down. If they can do it, so can you; you and your baby will both benefit.

How about alcohol?

Susan called my office in a panic. "I know I should be

happy," she said, "but I'm just so worried. I've read about the risks of alcohol causing birth defects, and I'm afraid my baby won't be normal. It took several months for me to get pregnant, and at first I didn't drink at all. But then when two months had passed and I still wasn't pregnant, I figured it would be all right to have a drink at a party last weekend. Well, actually, I had three glasses of wine, and now I've discovered I'm pregnant. What should I do?"

I suggested to Susan that she come in for an office visit the next day. Although I was aware from previous visits that Susan considered herself to be a "social drinker," I wanted to be sure I had accurate information about her drinking habits and that she had accurate information about the potential effects of alcohol on the developing fetus, so that she could make informed decisions about her drinking for the rest of her pregnancy.

The next day, after establishing that Susan was six weeks pregnant, we sat down to discuss her concerns. I emphasized that it was important to her and her baby to answer me honestly, and I asked her the following questions:

Do you drink beer? How many times a week? How much each time? Do you ever drink more?

Do you drink wine? How many times a week? How much each time? Do you ever drink more?

Do you drink hard liquor or mixed drinks? How often? How much? Do you ever drink more?

Susan's replies to these questions gave me a lot of information about her drinking habits. She did not drink beer. She was accustomed to drinking a couple of glasses of wine on the average of once a week, but she rarely consumed hard liquor. Since she found out she was pregnant, she had stopped drinking alcohol entirely.

This information allowed me to assure Susan that although her concern about drinking was valid, her guilt was not. While it is true that alcohol in large quantities is definitely harmful to a developing baby, any potential risks associated with smaller amounts are unproven. I suggested that rather than feeling guilty about her previous indulgence, she should concentrate on her desire to increase her chances of having a healthy baby by making informed choices about drinking in the future.

Alcohol is a drug that may cause serious problems in preg-nancy. It readily crosses the placenta; when the mother is drunk, so is the baby. It is well documented that the regular consumption of moderate to heavy amounts of alcoholic bev-erages can lead to lower birth weights and growth deficiencies, which may persist even after birth. Alcohol abuse is one of the three leading causes of birth defects and the only one of the three that is potentially preventable.

Research indicates that children born to women who are chronic alcoholics or heavy drinkers may be born with a con-dition known as *fetal alcohol syndrome*. Babies with fetal al-cohol syndrome often are underweight, malnourished, and small at birth and have characteristic facial features. They may have severe heart or limb abnormalities as well. Many of them have developmental delays and may be considered to be men-tally retarded. Although a baby with fetal alcohol syndrome may have severe defects and problems, some of the abnor-malities associated with the mother's drinking may be much more subtle.

It is not clear what effects the consumption of more mod-erate amounts of alcohol may have. Exact figures on the amount of alcohol that is harmful or required to produce fetal alcohol syndrome are not available. There is no doubt, however, that an average of six or more drinks per day is harmful; a drink is considered to be a twelve-ounce portion of beer, five ounces of wine, or one ounce of hard liquor.

Below that level, we do not know how much alcohol can be safely consumed. There is, of course, *no* risk of developing alcohol-related birth defects if the mother *abstains* from al-cohol. The U.S. Surgeon General, in a statement published in 1981, advised women who are pregnant (or considering pregnancy) not to drink alcoholic beverages and to be aware of the alcoholic content of food and drugs. Although this advice is obviously the safest course, it must be emphasized that we still cannot definitely conclude that occasionally consuming moderate amounts of alcohol during pregnancy is harmful.

There may be additional factors in the development of birth defects from alcohol. The fetus may be especially vulnerable to the effects of alcohol at a particular stage of pregnancy. Differences among individuals in their tolerance for and reactions to alcohol may play a part. There is also some suggestion that other birth-defect risk factors—such as smoking, the use of drugs, and poor nutrition—may compound the risks associated with alcohol consumption.

If a woman chooses to drink alcohol during pregnancy, many physicians recommend setting a two-drinks-per-day limit. There is some evidence that binge drinking—heavy, intermittent alcohol consumption—may be harmful, so it is not advisable for pregnant women to stop drinking for a week, only to "save up" for a big party.

It is also known that heavy drinkers who decrease their alcohol consumption during pregnancy lessen the risk for their babies. Therefore, a woman who has been drinking large amounts of alcohol during pregnancy should make an effort to cut down or stop drinking.

It seems prudent for all women who are pregnant or attempting to conceive to assess their lifestyles and habits honestly and realistically, including smoking, exercise, diet, and alcohol consumption.

A key point, however, is *honest* assessment. Many women with drinking problems tend to deny and minimize both the amounts they drink and the difficulties that their drinking has caused them. It may help to ask if drinking is *that* important and, if so, why? If a woman realizes she is drinking to deal with stress, alternative methods should be found. Pregnancy itself is frequently stressful, but drinking is certainly a nonproductive way to arrive at solutions to problems.

Women who drink "socially" should realize the potential effects of alcohol on their unborn child and should be encouraged to stop drinking or at least to cut down. A social occasion should not provide an excuse for overindulgence. If drinking is used as a way to deal with serious depression or major family financial or personal problems, it is important that counseling and treatment be sought. Alcohol-treatment centers exist in most major U.S. cities. Counselors, psychiatrists, psychologists, social workers, ministers, and other professionals can make a difference—not only in helping a woman with the personal problems that may lead to alcohol abuse but in helping her to change her drinking behavior so that her unborn child will have a better chance for a healthy beginning in life.

Remember, tobacco and alcohol are drugs. An unborn child cannot say no to a drink or a smoke. A pregnant woman must make the choice, not only for herself but for her child as well.

P.A.H.

# 13. If You Must Take Medicine

Most pregnant women want to do everything they can to ensure the well-being of their unborn children. Several of my patients have recently expressed concern that medications they take may harm their babies. Caution is indeed warranted. As the thalidomide story of the early 1960s so tragically illustrated, the placenta does not serve as a barrier that protects the fetus from the adverse effects of drugs used by the mother. It is important to keep in mind that when a pregnant woman is given a medication, two patients are being treated—and no substance has been proved to be 100 percent safe.

Two percent of live-born infants have major birth defects obvious from birth. Environmental factors, such as drug use, have been shown to cause 5 to 10 percent of these, and genetic problems are associated with another 25 percent of congenital abnormalities. Approximately 65 percent of these problems, however, are due to unidentifiable causes. Clearly, drug usage is not the only factor. Pregnant women are exposed to an ever-increasing number of substances that may affect the developing fetus. Food preservatives, insecticides, and polluted air and water are ever present and represent as-yet-unknown causative factors in birth defects.

A number of surveys in the United States and Europe have

revealed that the vast majority of pregnant women take some medication during pregnancy. Vitamins, iron, and pain relievers are the most frequently prescribed, followed by antacids, drugs to treat nausea and vomiting, antihistamines, and antibiotics. Most of these medications are generally considered beneficial and necessary rather than harmful.

The time during pregnancy when a drug is taken affects its potential for causing defects. For example, a drug taken in very early pregnancy, from fertilization to approximately day eighteen (about the time a woman first misses her menstrual period), is unlikely to cause a birth defect. If the drug is harmful to the fetus, it is more likely to cause a miscarriage than an abnormality.

Days 18 to 60 are the period of organ development. This is the time when the fetus is most sensitive to potential birth defects from drug use. Therefore, the first trimester is the time during which drug usage must be weighed most carefully. After day 60, the risk of a structural defect is reduced, but a medication may nonetheless affect fetal growth and development.

For some medical problems, the risk of no medication far outweighs the risk of potential abnormalities. For example, for many women who have a seizure disorder or epilepsy, uncontrolled seizures could cause a more severe problem for the fetus than the slightly increased risk of abnormalities that is known to be associated with some of the medications. However, for other women who are taking drugs for seizures but who have not had a seizure in many years, the medications can occasionally be stopped prior to pregnancy. The decision to stop medication is one that is closely examined by an obstetrician, in consultation with an internist, family physician, or neurologist, and should *not* be made by the woman herself.

The same type of consideration holds true for other medical conditions, such as high blood pressure, thyroid disorders, or psychiatric problems that are treated with drugs. In general, any woman with these problems should consult her physician for advice about the medication she takes *before* she becomes pregnant.

Acute conditions may also arise that pose a far greater risk than that of the medications used to treat them. Bladder infections, for example, are relatively common during pregnancy, and if they are not treated appropriately with antibiotics (usually penicillin or ampicillin), the infection can spread to the kidneys, causing a much more serious infection, which can even lead to premature labor.

It must be emphasized that no drug can be proved 100 percent safe, and that new research findings may emerge in the future. Advice to pregnant women to use or avoid any medication must be tempered by the available medical information. Aspirin in early pregnancy has not been shown to cause birth defects, and acetaminophen, a nonaspirin pain reliever, appears to be safe. Other drugs, such as tetracycline, which may cause permanent discoloration of the infant's teeth, should be avoided. For still other drugs, the answers are less clear. Women should seek the advice of their physicians about the use of medications during pregnancy, remembering that no guarantees about safety can honestly be made.

It's also important to remember that not every illness requires medication. The common cold is caused by a virus and cannot be "cured" by antibiotics or other drugs. The symptoms can be relieved somewhat by over-the-counter medications that are generally thought to be safe, but, if possible, it is better to deal with the symptoms without medication. Remember that over-the-counter substances are drugs, too.

Being careful about drugs during pregnancy, however, does not mean that taking a medication will inevitably cause birth defects. It also does not mean that a woman should refuse to take, or stop taking, a medication that has been prescribed for a valid medical reason. When in doubt, it's always best to discuss your questions with your doctor.

P.A.H.

# Part Three

❧

# A Trio of Special Situations

THUS FAR, WE'VE BEEN TALKING ABOUT WHAT EVERY MOTHER-to-be should know about her pregnancy and how best to assure the growth, development, and birth of a healthy child. But some pregnant women, and their obstetricians, need to take other factors into account. These pregnancies are "high-risk" pregnancies—not suggesting that an individual pregnancy is necessarily imperiled but that, statistically, a higher-than-average rate of complications has been recorded in such pregnancies.

Among the most prominent such situations are pregnancy after the age of thirty-five, pregnancy in women who are diabetic, and the conception of twins. If you are in one of these categories, your physician will take special pains to prevent problems and to be sure your pregnancy proceeds without untoward events. In the next three chapters, our obstetrician-authors explain today's ways of dealing with these special situations.

# 14. If You're Over 35

Many women are now marrying later and making conscious decisions about when to have children. Often, women have their schooling or careers to consider, and more couples are looking at the financial costs of a family and are waiting until they are better able to afford children. Some women have been trying to conceive but, because of fertility problems, have been previously unable to do so. Whatever the reasons, I am seeing more women in their thirties who are either pregnant or wish to conceive and who have questions about the risks to their health and that of their unborn children.

Nancy M. is a 32-year-old secretary with a six-year-old daughter. She was a new patient, and when I saw her for the first time, she seemed particularly anxious. As we explored her feelings about her second pregnancy, it became apparent that Nancy had some misconceptions. She very much wanted a second child but was concerned that she was too old. Most of her friends had completed their families when they were in their twenties. She told me that she had heard about amniocentesis and wanted to "have it done this week" so that she could be reassured that "everything was all right."

After I had established that Nancy's first child had been perfectly healthy and that there were no relatives with genetic illnesses, I explained that while amniocentesis can be a valuable test, it is not entirely without risk. I also explained that amniocentesis cannot give reassurances that *everything* is okay; it is not a universal screening test. I reassured Nancy that at age 32, her chances of having a healthy baby were excellent and that I would not consider her or her baby to be at particularly high risk because of her age.

Elinor D. is a 36-year-old lawyer who had been married for nine years. She came to see me for a routine annual checkup and requested that I remove her IUD. She and her husband had delayed having children until both had completed their schooling and were reasonably well established in their careers. Elinor told me she felt that if she was to have a child, it was "now or never." She recognized that having a child would require many changes in their lifestyle, but both she and her husband were willing to make those changes for the sake of a family. She had also read about the increased risk of chromosomal abnormalities in infants born to women over 35.

We discussed the need for early prenatal care when she did conceive, and I explained that I would recommend genetic counseling and amniocentesis as the pregnancy progressed. I emphasized that because she had been healthy, I did not anticipate any special problems with her pregnancy. Prenatal care is in many ways a form of preventive medicine, and I told Elinor that I would be trying to anticipate any potential problems that might be associated with her age.

Although a 35-year-old woman can hardly be called old, if she is pregnant for the first time, she is called, in medical terms, an *elderly primigravida*. Certainly no woman enjoys being called elderly, but the term has served to emphasize that pregnancy for women in that age group has been considered high-risk by the medical profession. And although many women over 35 have given birth to normal babies, there are some valid health considerations associated with aging that must be discussed.

Many studies indicate that the risk of genetic and chromosomal abnormalities does increase with the mother's age. Up to age 35, the risk of having a baby with a chromosomal abnormality is quite small. At that age, the risk is approximately 0.6 percent, or a 99.4 percent chance of having an infant with no chromosomal abnormality. At age 40, the risk increases to a 1.6 percent chance of an abnormality, and at age 45, a 5.4 percent chance.

The most common of these problems is Down's syndrome. There are tests, performed between the fifteenth and twentieth weeks of pregnancy, that can detect Down's syndrome as well as some other serious birth defects. These tests, which include amniocentesis and ultrasound, will reassure the majority of parents that their unborn baby is free from most chromosomal problems.

*Amniocentesis*, in which a sample of amniotic fluid is withdrawn from the uterus through a needle inserted into the mother's abdomen, is usually a safe procedure, but there is a small risk—less than 1 percent—of miscarriage or serious complication associated with it. Because of that small risk, physicians will generally not recommend amniocentesis if the chance of having a chromosomal problem is felt to be less than the risk of the testing procedure. Most physicians, however, will counsel women 35 and over about amniocentesis.

Because labor has been likened to an athletic performance, it has been suggested that the capacity to undertake labor efficiently declines with increasing age. The incidence of first cesarean section is reported to be significantly greater in women over 35. This may be partially attributable to *dysfunctional labor* (labor that does not progress properly), increased incidence of diabetes and high blood pressure, bleeding abnormalities, or fetal distress, all of which can necessitate delivery by cesarean section.

It is also possible that obstetricians may use different criteria when deciding the mode of delivery for those women they consider to be at high risk. The concept of "premium pregnancy," perhaps the only or last pregnancy an older woman will experience, may contribute to a greater willingness for an obstetrician to perform a cesarean.

There are other health considerations of which women who are delaying pregnancy should be aware. The incidence of chronic medical conditions such as diabetes and high blood pressure increases with age, and pregnant women with any of these problems are considered to be at high risk no matter how old they are. There is a possibility of infertility associated with previous severe uterine and tubal infections, endometriosis, and uterine fibroids. *Fibroids*, muscular tumors of the uterine wall, may develop and increase in size as a woman grows older and may result in difficulty conceiving or carrying a pregnancy to term, although the majority of women with fibroids do not have these problems.

It is important to note that the assessment of pregnancy in women over 35 as a high-risk situation is based primarily on retrospective reviews of past occurrences. One recent study at Grady Memorial Hospital in Atlanta concluded that age *alone* did *not* appear to be an important risk factor for healthy pregnant women in this age group. But not all studies support that conclusion.

It makes sense to consider that we are all gradually aging and to look realistically at the implications for pregnant women over 35. A woman contemplating pregnancy should be aware of the availability of genetic testing and should seek prenatal care as soon as she suspects she is pregnant.

Most physicians will counsel women over 35 about ultrasound and amniocentesis. Because such testing involves specialized personnel, including genetics counselors and obstetricians experienced in amniocentesis, as well as ultrasound facilities and a genetics laboratory, such prenatal genetic diagnosis is best performed in a major medical center or teaching hospital.

P.A.H.

# 15. If You're Diabetic

When I was a junior in medical school, I attended a lecture on diabetes in pregnancy at the same time that Carol P., a diabetic friend, was pregnant with her first child.

Carol was 23; she had been diabetic since she was nine years old. In spite of having been diabetic for fourteen years, her health seemed good. Her emotional outlook was bright. She gave herself an insulin injection every morning and then went about her daily activities like any other young wife.

Dr. William Given, who was then a young professor and an excellent teacher, was the lecturer. He was proud to report to his eager students that experience in diabetic-pregnancy management had improved the success rate, so that fetal mortality was down to 25 percent. Dr. Given turned out to be Carol's obstetrician, and my first experiences with diabetic pregnancies were gained by watching Carol's pregnancy progress and by hearing what her problems were.

In those days, the diabetic pregnant woman was examined every two weeks by either her obstetrician or her internist, often a diabetes specialist. Obstetrician and internist usually alternated these two-week visits. They would occasionally check blood sugar and adjust the daily insulin dosage. In addition, the pregnant diabetic checked her own urine sugar and made small adjustments in her insulin dosage as needed.

There were two main problems in the management of the diabetic pregnancy in those days. Both problems were related to the placenta.

First, the pregnant diabetic had an increased chance of developing *toxemia of pregnancy*, also called *eclampsia*. This is a condition in which the mother's blood pressure rises, she retains fluid and becomes swollen, and her kidneys begin to work inefficiently, causing her to lose *albumin*—a protein— via her urine. Eclampsia is due to the placenta's becoming diseased and producing abnormal products. If eclampsia is not diagnosed and treated promptly, it can progress to convulsions and possibly the mother's death.

The placenta of a diabetic woman can also fail in the transport of oxygen and nutrients to the baby. In those days, there were no tests of placental function. It was not unusual for the diabetic woman to have a perfectly healthy fetus one day, and for the baby to die in the uterus the next day because the placenta stopped working adequately. The longer the diabetic's pregnancy progressed, the more likely that a tragic end would occur.

It was known that if the fetus remained in the uterus for more than 36 weeks, it ran a seriously increasing risk of dying because of placental malfunction. If delivery occurred before that point, however, the baby had a greater chance of dying from the complications of prematurity. The most common of such complications was *respiratory distress syndrome* (RDS), a condition of reduced lung development, which is more common in diabetics' babies. The best time for delivery, then, would be at precisely 36 weeks.

Since it is usually very difficult to induce labor for the first delivery at 36 weeks, Carol was scheduled for a cesarean section. Carol knew that the baby would have a 25 percent chance of dying. It required a great deal of bravery for a diabetic woman to become a mother in those days.

Carol's daughter, Danielle, is 25 years old now, and she has graduated from law school.

That brings us to the present. The story is altogether different now. Last year, Madeline C. came to me for the care of her first pregnancy. Madeline was 28 years old, and she had been a diabetic for sixteen years.

I explained to her that the survival rate of babies born to diabetic mothers is now 97 percent—closely approaching that of nondiabetics' babies. But Madeline would need much closer supervision than the normal pregnant woman. We would employ many new and special tests.

In the 1960s, it had been shown that tight control of diabetes is essential to help prevent toxemia and for normal development of the fetus. This means that the blood sugar would have to be as close to normal levels as possible. The latest findings indicate that a diabetic woman's blood-sugar level should be tightly controlled before she gets pregnant, so it is best if she plans her pregnancy.

Madeline would have her blood sugar monitored at my office or her internist's every week and, in addition, she was taught to test her own blood sugar at home every day. Home glucose meters and glucose test strips, which enable patients to test their own blood sugars easily, have come on the market just within the last couple of years. (Some diabetic patients, however, require hospitalization in early pregnancy to achieve this measure of control.)

From her thirtieth week of pregnancy, I started to examine Madeline every week. Each time, she had nonstress testing of the fetus; this measures the fetal heart rate in relation to fetal movement. When the fetal heart speeds up with fetal movement, it means that the placenta is healthy and the baby is not in danger.

At 36 weeks, Madeline was hospitalized. Our goal now was to get maximum time in the uterus for the baby, while making sure that the placenta wasn't failing. We tested the fetal heart every three days.

In addition, we monitored the output of a hormone called *estriol*. Estriol is produced by the healthy placenta and is excreted in the mother's urine. If estriol levels drop, we have a sign that the placenta is failing.

At 38 weeks, we performed an amniocentesis. Since the early 1970s, we have known that fetal lung maturity can be demonstrated by testing for two fatty substances, called *lecithin* and *sphingomyelin*, in the amniotic fluid. This is called the *L/S ratio test*. The L/S ratio of Madeline's amniotic fluid showed that the lungs had developed sufficiently that the baby was not in danger of developing RDS, should it have to be delivered now.

This proved to be fortunate indeed, for later that day, the laboratory reported that the urinary estriol had dropped. We immediately did a fetal heart test. It confirmed that the placenta was failing; we were running out of time. And we had to deliver the baby quickly.

Madeline underwent an induction of labor that very evening. By now, her cervix had softened enough that we could safely try an induction. We would use electronic fetal monitoring to be sure that the labor would not hurt the baby. We were prepared to do an immediate cesarean section if the monitor showed that the fetus could not tolerate labor.

Because of the scientific advances of the past twenty years, infants of diabetic mothers have an excellent chance of survival. But the pride that I felt as a doctor when I delivered Madeline's baby was surpassed by Madeline's own pride in her new daughter. By some strange coincidence, she was named Danielle.

G.G.P.

# 16. If You're Expecting Twins

"My response to being a twin myself and now having twins was mostly one of surprise," says Margaret D. "My husband is very excited and pleased. I think that the reason for my surprise is that while I have been reading up on childbirth, I have been deliberately skipping the chapters on multiple births. Maybe it's because I didn't want to face it."

I had suspected that Margaret was having twins when I saw her for her third prenatal visit; she was then sixteen weeks pregnant. When I felt her abdomen, I expected to find the uterus about two finger widths below the *umbilicus* (navel). Much to my surprise, however, the uterus was at the umbilicus itself—the size for a twenty-weeks pregnancy.

We reviewed the date of her last menstrual period. Margaret remembered that it was a perfectly normal period, like others. There seemed no chance that she was actually further along in her pregnancy than the dates themselves predicted.

I asked her if she had felt any fetal movement, and she answered that she had not. Most pregnant women first feel movement at eighteen weeks of pregnancy. Therefore, with Margaret's uterus being the twenty-weeks size, and without her having felt movement, we had evidence that the uterus was larger than expected for the development of a single fetus.

I sent Margaret for a sonogram, to study the uterus and its contents. *Sonography* is a technique that was developed for use in obstetrics in the 1970s. Intermittent high-frequency sound waves are generated at the end of a wandlike arm that is passed over the part of the body being studied—in this case, the abdomen. When the sound waves passing into the body strike a surface between objects of different densities, they send back reflections. The sound waves would pass through the amniotic fluid and would reflect back from the baby. An oscilloscope screen, much like a television screen, displays the reflections as an outline. When Margaret had her sonography done, the outlines of two babies appeared. We had established the diagnosis of twins.

In the United States, twins occur once in every 84 births, with the frequency varying among different races. One set of twins occurs in every 93 births to white Americans, while in black Americans, a set of twins occurs in every 78 births. Twinning among Orientals is less common. In Japan, for example, twins occur only once in every 155 births.

Most twins result from the fertilization of two separate ova (eggs) that are produced at about the same time in a single ovulation cycle. The rarity of two eggs being produced in the same cycle is the reason for the rarity of twins. Twins that occur due to the fertilization of two separate ova are called *fraternal twins*.

About one-third as often, twins are formed from the fertilization of a single ovum. After fertilization, for reasons we don't know, the fertilized egg divides into two similar parts. Each section will go on to develop into a separate embryo. Twins formed in this way are *identical twins*. Identical twins occur independently of race, heredity, or age. The statistics for this sort of twinning are the same around the world: One set of identical twins occurs in every 250 births.

Fraternal twinning is not only racially dependent but also seems to be hereditary. It has been found that women who are fraternal twins themselves give birth to twins once in every 58 pregnancies. (If the father is a fraternal twin, the chance of twins occurring is only once in 126 pregnancies.)

Since Margaret was a fraternal twin herself, I expected that the twins she was carrying would also be fraternal twins.

On her next visit, Margaret said, "I think that twins struggle. I've often tried to imagine what it must be like in a womb for two little ones. I was trying to figure out how the placenta feeds two. Is it split?"

At the beginning of most twin pregnancies, there are usually two placentas, one for each fetus. But Margaret had excellent insight into the intrauterine life of twins. There is a constant struggle for nutrients and for space. As the pregnancy progresses, space becomes so limited that the placentas are pushed against each other until they fuse. By the time of birth, most twins share one placenta.

Although the twins are in separate amniotic sacs, they get pushed against each other. As the pregnancy progresses and the uterus grows as much as it is able, the pressure causes the membranes to bulge and press down against the cervix, causing the cervix to become thin and to dilate before it would normally do so. Thus, the mother carrying twins is at risk of premature labor.

The average duration of pregnancy for twin births is 37 weeks, compared with the normal 40 weeks for single births. Twins, then, tend to be born earlier and to be smaller than single babies. Half of all twins weigh less than 2,500 grams (five and a half pounds) and are premature babies.

I outlined for Margaret the defensive strategy we would employ to improve her twins' chances for maximum growth and development. She was warned, for one thing, not to smoke at all, since smoking causes infants to grow more slowly. Every lost ounce would be precious if the twins were born prematurely.

I told Margaret, too, that she must not have sexual intercourse, or *any* sexual activity, from the sixth month on. Sexual excitement causes uterine contractions, which would increase the downward pressure against the cervix.

She was also given iron supplements and extra vitamins, and we reviewed her nutrition carefully. We particularly wanted to be sure that her protein intake was high, to meet the double requirements of twins.

Margaret was placed on daily rest periods in bed from the sixth month to the middle of the eighth month. By resting in bed, the blood flow to the uterus is increased; this carries increased nutrients to the now-fused placenta and permits more efficient removal of waste products. And, of course, the horizontal position in bed reduces the force against the cervix.

From the thirty-fourth week on, Margaret was kept in bed all day, except for meals and bathroom visits. And the twins grew and developed.

She went into labor at 38 weeks and, fortunately, was able

to have an uncomplicated vaginal delivery. (Some patients are not as fortunate, for certain complications may occur with twin labors. Sometimes, for example, the twins can become interlocked so that a cesarean section must be done.)

Fraternal twin girls were delivered; one weighed six pounds and the other six and a half pounds. Margaret told me, "We love them both, but I think I will try to make a special effort to help the smaller one." The most important special efforts for twins, though, are those expended *before* they are born.

G.G.P.

# Part Four

ᴥ

# Inside Tracking

Tʜᴇ ᴍᴀɪɴ ǫᴜᴇsᴛɪᴏɴ ɪɴ ᴛʜᴇ ᴍɪɴᴅ ᴏꜰ ᴀ ᴍᴏᴛʜᴇʀ-ᴛᴏ-ʙᴇ, ᴀɴᴅ in that of her physician or nurse-midwife as well, is, of course: How is the baby doing? Is the fetus developing normally? Is it growing at the rate it should? It would be wonderful to have a "window" that would allow a peek inside; if the mother's abdomen could be magically rendered transparent every once in a while, a watchful eye could be kept on the baby-to-be.

Since that's impossible, medicine has looked for other ways to gauge fetal progress and to detect difficulties. Some are as simple as the mother's sense of movement within her womb; others, referred to briefly in some of the preceding chapters, are sophisticated achievements of twentieth-century technology. The next four chapters review the major techniques modern medicine uses to follow the unseen events inside the uterus.

# 17. Fetal Movement

Many pregnant women wonder about the significance of their babies' movements. They sense different types of movement and periods of quiet. They worry if the pattern of their babies' movements changes.

Most women feel their babies move for the first time at about eighteen weeks of pregnancy. But this important milestone doesn't check exactly for all pregnant women. The fetus actually begins to make spontaneous movements at about eleven weeks of pregnancy, but most women do not feel these faint and feeble movements. In fact, many women don't feel the first movement of the fetus until later than the eighteenth week, and many movements occurring thereafter are not felt by the mother at all. The number of fetal movements an individual woman feels is related to her sensitivity and to the characteristic vigor of her particular fetus.

One group of British researchers, for example, compared movements felt by 40 women, 25 to 40 weeks pregnant, with movements measured by ultrasound. They found that ultrasound recordings showed an average of 60 movements in 45 minutes—but the mothers sensed an average of only 31 movements over the same time period. Each woman felt a certain percentage of her baby's movements, and that percentage was relatively constant for that particular woman and her pregnancy.

Using an electromechanical method, Dr. E. Sadovsky of Hadassah University Hospital in Jerusalem has studied the pattern of fetal movement throughout pregnancy as well as the range of patterns for individual women. He found that the average number of daily fetal movements recorded rose from about 200 in the twentieth week to 500 in the thirty-second week. Then it gradually decreased until delivery, to a mean of under 300. The number of daily fetal movements ranged from 50 to over 950. But even women with low daily figures, if those levels were constant, delivered normal infants.

Dr. Sadovsky also investigated the pregnant women's own

measurements of movement for 30 to 60 minutes, two to three times a day. He found that the patients could sense about 87 percent of the motions (as compared with about 50 percent of the motions recorded in the British study).

The fetus shows its own general characteristic pattern of movement, which may be mild or vigorous—and many pregnant women report that their babies "sleep," although so far, no study has documented this. In addition, the movement may be stimulated in various ways. Most pregnant women discover that by gently tapping the abdominal wall they can stimulate increased fetal movements.

The fetus will also respond to external sound with increased movement, particularly if the sound is loud. Few pregnant women can sit through a rock concert without feeling uncomfortable due to the increased rate and vigor of their babies' movements.

Light, too, will stimulate the fetus. Dr. Sadovsky found that shining a 250-watt bulb for twenty minutes over a pregnant woman's abdomen will increase fetal movement in two out of three normal pregnancies.

Fetal movements usually slow down during the few days prior to the onset of labor. While no one has proved precisely why this reduction of movement takes place, it is believed to be due to the diminishing uterine volume. During the few days prior to the onset of labor, uterine muscle tone increases and the uterine volume shrinks slightly. Perhaps the baby no longer has enough room for forceful movements to be made.

This effect becomes even more noticeable with the start of labor. After rupture of the membranes, the uterus contracts down even more, further limiting the fetal kicks. Forceful movement of the baby is so rare at this time that a nurse or a doctor who examines your abdomen during active labor and feels a movement will invariably be surprised.

Recently, obstetricians have started to monitor the fetal heart rate changes that occur in response to its movements. This is done by fetal heart rate monitoring. Fetal heart rate monitoring during labor has for some time contributed to preventing damage or loss of the baby, and the obstetrician or midwife has always listened to the fetal heart during your prenatal visits. But now, by correlating the fetal heart rate with the movement of the baby, a new test for fetal well-being has evolved. This test is called the *nonstress test,* or *NST*. Its name distinguishes the NST from the *contraction stress test,* or *CST*.

In the CST, the fetal heart rate is monitored and watched as contractions of the uterus take place. The uterine contractions often occur spontaneously, or they can be made to occur by giving a contraction-causing hormone to the mother. If the fetal heart rate drops slightly after a uterine contraction, that is a danger signal revealing that the baby and the placenta are functioning at a less-than-normal level.

The NST monitors the fetal heart rate and studies the effect of the baby's movements on its heart rate. If the heart rate speeds up as a response to fetal movement, that is called a *reactive pattern,* and it is a sign of fetal well-being.

Dr. Barry S. Schifrin and his associates in the obstetrics and gynecology department of the Cedars-Sinai Medical Center in Los Angeles studied more than 4,500 antepartum nonstress tests in the late 1970s. They found that fetuses with reactive NSTs were more likely to display normal fetal heart rate patterns during labor and had a lower chance of having fetal distress or other problems during labor and delivery. They concluded that the reactive NST not only depicts fetal well-being at the time of the test, but also has a predictive value for fetal well-being during labor and delivery.

In-depth studies of fetal movement and its significance are relatively new, but the prudent pregnant woman can follow some general guidelines. By the start of the seventh month, you should have a good instinctive feeling for the normal movement pattern of your baby. If, at any time, you believe that there is a reduction of fetal movement from the usual pattern, lie down in a quiet place. Evaluate the movement. If indeed the pattern has changed, tell your doctor, who can perform the tests that are necessary to define the baby's health further.

G.G.P.

# 18. Ultrasound

As recently as the late 1960s, ultrasound was a research tool available only in major medical centers. Today, many obstetricians are purchasing portable ultrasound machines for office use, and most community hospitals have an ultrasound machine available. Although it is also used in other areas of medicine, ultrasound has become an important diagnostic tool in gynecology and obstetrics because it can provide some of the same information as an X ray without the risks of exposure to radiation.

Ultrasound is a medical technique in which high-frequency sound waves are aimed at the area of the body to be examined—in a pregnant woman, the uterus. These sound waves, which are inaudible to the human ear, are generated by a specially designed ultrasound transducer and are then reflected, or bounced back, at different rates, depending on the density of the tissue being examined.

In diagnostic ultrasound, the reflected sound waves are transformed into electrical signals and displayed as an image on a screen. Since fluid reflects very few sound waves, such an area appears black; bone reflects many more sound waves and shows up as white areas on the screen. The image formed may appear to be only shadows of light and dark to someone inexperienced in viewing ultrasound pictures, but to an obstetrician or radiologist familiar with the technique, much information can be gained. Occasionally, a clear profile view of the fetus will allow the mother to recognize facial features or even the baby sucking its thumb.

An ultrasound examination (sonogram) is a painless procedure. A small probe or wand is pressed gently back and forth across the abdomen, which has been lubricated with a conducting gel or oil. One mildly uncomfortable aspect of most obstetrical ultrasound exams is the need to maintain a full bladder. (Four or five glasses of water or juice are usually enough to fill the bladder and produce the feeling of having to urinate.) A full bladder serves several purposes: It may elevate the fetal head so that the head can be accurately measured, and it also provides a clear "window" through which the structures behind the bladder (the cervix and lower uterine segment) can be better outlined and visualized.

Obstetrical ultrasound has many applications, but it is most often used to determine the gestational age of the fetus. Some women may be unsure of the date of their last menstrual period, and the pelvic examination may reveal that the uterus is either smaller or larger than expected. A sonogram can resolve the question of how far along the pregnancy actually is. Some medical problems, such as diabetes, affect the rate of fetal growth, and repeated ultrasound exams are useful in monitoring the fetus's development. It is also necessary to ascertain the gestational age of the fetus if a woman is going to have a cesarean section, so that delivery can be appropriately timed. Likewise, knowing the gestational age of the fetus is important for women with high blood pressure or diabetes, since a preterm delivery may be necessary.

Gestational age can be determined by one of two kinds of measurements: fetal crown-rump length or biparietal diameter. Between eight and twelve weeks, the fetal crown-rump length can indicate gestational age within an accuracy range of plus or minus five days. It is more difficult to obtain a precise measurement between twelve and sixteen weeks; the fetus is usually in a more curled position, so readings during this time tend to be less accurate.

From about the beginning of the second trimester, the biparietal diameter—the largest transverse diameter of the fetal head—serves as an indicator of gestational age that is accurate to plus or minus eleven days. As the pregnancy progresses past about 26 weeks, these measurements become gradually less accurate, so that beyond 32 weeks, an estimate of gestational age can be made accurate only to within about three weeks.

Ultrasound is also useful for other purposes—in diagnosing twins, for example. Before ultrasound was available, as many as 50 percent of mothers who give birth to twins did not know they were carrying twins until the time of delivery. A sonogram can be used to diagnose multiple gestations in plenty of time for both obstetrician and parents to prepare for the births.

Some birth defects that affect the size or anatomy of the fetal organs or limbs (hydrocephalus, kidney cysts, fetal tumors, certain heart defects and spinal abnormalities, and some defects that cause limb shortening, for example) can show up on a sonogram as well. Ultrasound examinations can also be used to diagnose other potentially dangerous conditions, such as placenta previa, a condition in which the placenta covers all or part of the cervix, the mouth of the uterus. Placenta previa often necessitates a cesarean delivery, and an ultrasound scan enables an obstetrician to determine the exact location of the placenta and plan for this high-risk situation.

Amniocentesis, which involves inserting a fine needle into the uterus to remove amniotic fluid for testing, may be necessary in some pregnancies. Ultrasound is used to find the best site for inserting the needle in order to avoid the fetus and the placenta.

Another bit of information a sonogram may provide is the sex of the fetus. This is certainly not a reason for doing the test, and the ability to visualize a male fetus's scrotum depends on the baby's position in the uterus and the ultrasonographer's skill. Many physicians or technicians who perform ultrasound exams are reluctant to comment on this information, since even the most skilled examiners are not 100 percent accurate in diagnosing the sex of the fetus.

How safe is ultrasound? As with any medical test, the safety of the procedure is an important consideration. Research concerning the effects of ultrasound on human tissue is continuing. Many studies have explored the effects of ultrasound on individual cells or on animals, and some of them have attributed such possibly adverse effects as temperature changes or chromosomal changes within the cells to ultrasound.

Many other studies, including a survey of the effects of ultrasound on over 10,000 women in Manitoba, Canada, have found no evidence that ultrasound endangers the fetus or the mother, although there was a slight suggestion of lower birth weight in those infants exposed to ultrasound during their gestation. Caution must be used in interpreting these results, however, since ultrasound exams were performed more frequently for high-risk pregnancies.

In other studies, the frequency of the ultrasound waves and the duration of exposure may be vastly different from the exposure levels in actual diagnostic ultrasound examinations. Although the possibility exists that repeated exposure of the fetus to ultrasound may carry potential risks, there is no conclusive evidence to date of adverse effects.

Today, some obstetricians feel that the potential risks are so low that a sonogram would be useful for every pregnant woman. Others feel that although no risks have been demonstrated in over fifteen years of use, the procedure should be reserved for those situations in which the information gained would be necessary for the appropriate medical care of both mother and baby.

P.A.H.

# 19. Amniocentesis

Amniocentesis is the process by which a small sample of the amniotic fluid in which the unborn child floats is removed from the uterus for analysis. Studying the amniotic fluid permits diagnosis of a number of conditions or diseases of the fetus while it is still in the uterus.

The technique of removing amniotic fluid through the abdomen of the mother has been known for over 100 years. But only within the past 15 to 25 years has amniocentesis been able to monitor midtrimester pregnancies at risk for specific types of birth defects. And thousands of women at risk for birth-defective children can now undergo pregnancies with good assurance of a happy outcome and a normal baby.

Amniotic fluid looks much like urine. In fact, its major component is the urine of the fetus. It contains many cells that have been shed by the baby and the sac of membranes as part of their normal development. The amniotic fluid also contains hormones and chemicals such as proteins and salts. By analyzing both the cells and the various chemicals, much information can be gathered about fetal well-being.

The biochemical studies of the fluid can be performed immediately, but the cell analysis takes many weeks. The cells, which are microscopic, must be cultured, a very delicate procedure by which the fetal cells are grown into colonies of their own clones.

Since the cells in amniotic fluid are discarded cells from the fetus, only about 20 percent are still alive when the culture is attempted. This is analogous to trying to produce a good harvest in your garden when only one-fifth of the seeds are viable. For this reason, not all culture attempts are successful, and some women—about one out of twenty—must undergo amniocentesis a second time.

At harvest time, the cells can be analyzed biochemically, as one might do in families that have a history of rare enzyme deficiencies. But most amniocentesis is performed to see if there are any extra, missing, or abnormal chromosomes. Chromosomes are microscopic structures that carry genes, specific protein molecules that are the determinants of the function and traits of the resulting organism—in this case, the baby.

In humans, there are normally 23 pairs of chromosomes in each cell, for a total of 46. Chromosomes look something like short, bent twigs under the microscope. The bends and shapes enable each pair to be identified, from pair number one to pair number 23. That last pair determines the child's sex. If you are undergoing amniocentesis for chromosomal analysis, a fringe benefit is that you can learn the sex of the child before it is born, if you wish.

But the main reason for this analysis is to detect chromosomal abnormalities. Twenty-five percent of congenital defects are due to chromosomal abnormalities, and if severe abnormalities are found in early pregnancy, the parents may have the option of abortion.

For reasons not yet defined, chromosomal abnormalities become more common in older pregnant women, and 90 percent of the chromosomal abnormalities are due to a condition known as *trisomy 21,* or *Down's syndrome* (formerly sometimes known as "mongolism"). This condition is associated with various degrees of mental retardation, disorders of body form, and often serious defects of internal organs such as the heart. In Down's syndrome, there are three number 21 chromosomes instead of just a pair—hence, the name trisomy 21.

The fact that chromosomal abnormalities become more common as women get older becomes an important factor in the decision as to whether or not to undergo amniocentesis. Ernest B. Hook of the New York State Department of Health reported this analysis of maternal age rates of Down's syndrome in *The Lancet*, a leading British medical journal:

| MATERNAL AGE | INCIDENCE OF DOWN'S SYNDROME |
|:---:|:---:|
| 34 | 1 in 527 |
| 35 | 1 in 413 |
| 36 | 1 in 333 |
| 37 | 1 in 266 |
| 38 | 1 in 183 |
| 39 | 1 in 135 |
| 40 | 1 in 106 |
| 41 | 1 in 83 |

Advanced maternal age, then, is the most frequent indication for amniocentesis. And if a previous child was affected by Down's syndrome, there is a recurrence risk of one in 60, not associated with age.

Amniocentesis is usually performed at about the sixteenth week of pregnancy. (Prior to that time, the amount of amniotic fluid is so small that it is difficult to get a proper sample.) The mother lies on her back, her lower abdomen is cleansed, and a local anesthetic is injected. A long, thin needle is passed through the lower abdominal wall into the uterus and the amniotic sac. The passage of the needle is usually monitored by a sonography scanner, which shows the outline of the baby. This is to help the doctor avoid sticking the baby with the needle.

About one ounce of fluid is removed from the cupful of amniotic fluid present in the uterus at that time. The procedure is usually tolerated well.

Then why should not all pregnant women have amniocentesis? The reason is that there is a small but definite risk to the fetus. In the late 1970s, a number of studies were published from amniocentesis centers in the United States, Australia, Scandinavia, and Israel. In five separate studies, risk factors ranged between 1.5 and 5 percent. No mothers died, but most doctors now agree that there is a risk of fetal loss of about 1 to 2 percent, due to miscarriage following amniocentesis.

The decision as to whether or not to undergo amniocentesis is yours to make. You must balance your feelings and the risk factors related to your medical history and your age. It is an intensely personal decision.

G.G.P.

# 20. The Alpha-Fetoprotein Test

During the past twenty years, there have been great advances in fetal testing, testing performed to evaluate fetal health and well-being. Most such tests have no risks. Some do have risks associated with them, however, and they must be evaluated for each pregnant woman and her baby before the test is done. There is one test that has no risk when it is performed, yet poses a potential threat to each baby whose mother has the test—the alpha-fetoprotein blood test.

I have performed this blood test on all of my pregnant patients at about fourteen to sixteen weeks' gestation for the past five years; yet each time, I dread the possibility that the result will be abnormal, for the interpretation is not straightforward. The follow-up investigation of an abnormal test result subjects the baby to risks and the parents to insecurity and serious worry. It may even lead some parents and obstetricians to abort normal babies.

*Alpha-fetoprotein (AFP)* is the protein, mostly produced by the fetal liver, that constitutes the major factor in fetal blood serum. No significant amount of AFP is normally found in an adult, but during pregnancy, the level of AFP in the mother's blood rises somewhat; this is quite normal and expected. The

AFP probably enters the amniotic fluid in the fetal urine, crosses the membranes, and enters the mother's circulation.

Sometimes, however, a higher-than-expected level is found. There are two possible sources for this. First, blood containing AFP might leak out from tiny breaks that can occur normally in placental blood vessels and enter the maternal circulation across the placenta. Second, and more important, fetal blood serum containing AFP can leak into the amniotic fluid from an open defect in the fetus's brain or spinal column and cross the fetal membranes into the mother's blood. Consequently, when AFP is found in an abnormally high concentration in a pregnant woman's blood, such a condition, called a *neural tube defect,* is suspected.

I recently discussed this problem with Dr. Hart Peterson, associate professor of pediatrics at Cornell University Medical College in New York City. He pointed out that one-half of the babies with open neural tube defects are *anencephalics*—babies with defective skulls and brains—who cannot survive more than a few days after birth. The rest have some form of *spina bifida,* a defective spinal column with external bulging of a saclike structure containing spinal membranes and sometimes the spinal cord. In the United States, the incidence of fetuses with neural tube defects is about two in every 1,000.

In Great Britain, where neural tube defects are more common, a wide-scale AFP blood screening study was conducted in the mid-1970s on almost 20,000 pregnant women. Nearly 90 percent of the women who had anencephalic fetuses, and 80 percent of those whose babies had spina bifida, had had markedly elevated blood levels of AFP at sixteen to eighteen weeks' gestation. But among the women with high AFP levels were many who gave birth to normal infants.

Because these "false-positive" test results are so common, blood AFP levels cannot be used for diagnosis, but only to identify the high-risk group. Estimates of the number of women with abnormally high blood AFP levels who actually have a baby with an open neural tube defect vary from one in ten to about one in 30.

Women with markedly elevated AFP must undergo further

testing; both ultrasound and amniocentesis may be used. An experienced sonographer can often identify anencephalic fetuses and may be able to detect some cases of spina bifida. Ultrasound diagnosis may also reveal other causes for high AFP levels: Twin gestation, fetal death, and error in estimating fetal age are among them.

Amniocentesis can be used to measure the level of the AFP in the amniotic fluid itself. But we thus reach a point where a simple blood test subjects many normal babies to additional testing, which may carry some risk, to detect the few abnormal babies. So we must carefully analyze the benefits of these riskier tests.

Dr. Aubrey Milunsky of Harvard Medical School reported his experiences with amniotic AFP studies of 20,000 pregnancies in the *Journal of the American Medical Association* in 1980. Of the 334 cases of raised AFP level in the amniotic fluid, about 40 percent of the fetuses had open neural tube defects; 27 percent had other defects or abnormal conditions; and 32 percent were normal, the raised level of AFP in these cases usually explainable by contamination of the amniotic fluid with fetal red blood cells during the amniocentesis process. In this study, no open neural tube defects were missed, but eleven of the women who had their pregnancies terminated because of the AFP test actually had normal fetuses.

Dr. James N. Macri, assistant professor of obstetrics and gynecology at the School of Medicine, State University of New York at Stony Brook, and Robert R. Weiss, M.D., have reported the results of a program screening more than 17,000 women for blood AFP levels. Nearly 4 percent had significantly elevated levels, and, after further screening, amniocentesis was performed on about 2 percent. Of those 365 women, 36 had a raised AFP level in the amniotic fluid; twenty of these fetuses had open neural tube defects, eight had other abnormalities, and eight were normal. Because of careful reexamination of these 36 women, no normal pregnancies were terminated.

In considering follow-up testing of a woman with elevated blood levels of AFP, we should recall that about half of the affected babies will have anencephaly, which can often be diagnosed by sonography alone, and that spina bifida can sometimes be detected by a skilled sonographer.

When I find a patient with an elevated blood AFP level, I explain to the parents that they probably have a one in 30 chance of having an abnormal baby, and I will recommend sonography as the next step. Each decision about AFP testing is accompanied by complex ethical issues that must be discussed in detail.

G.G.P.

# Part Five

❧

# Eleven
# Not-Uncommon
# Problems

IT IS TO BE HOPED THAT YOUR PREGNANCY WILL BE ONE OF the kind medicine describes as "unremarkable"—nothing unusual, nothing requiring special medical intervention—and will proceed smoothly to its happy culmination. Unfortunately, that does not always happen. Distinctly untoward events may occasionally complicate that expected course.

While such events do not occur in the majority of pregnancies, they are by no means rare. Some may threaten the mother, others the baby, still others both. Should such an event occur, you will want to know everything possible about the reasons and possible remedies. The information in the next eleven chapters is, of necessity, general. Each case is, of course, individual—and if there seems to be a conflict of opinion, you should follow your own physician's advice.

# 21. Accidents

A pregnant woman is especially vulnerable to accidents—luckily, usually minor ones, such as falls. Barbara M., 26 years old and pregnant for the first time, recently described such a fall to me: "I feel like such an idiot. Now that I'm pregnant, I'm always bumping into things. Last week, I had to go into a store to use the bathroom. There was one step; under normal circumstances, I would have seen it, but I fell right over it. My elbow really hurt, but all I could think was, 'Did I hurt the baby?' The police took me to the hospital; they X-rayed my elbow and it was okay, and they put me on a fetal monitor for two hours, and the baby was okay, too."

There are several reasons a pregnant woman tends to be accident-prone. First, there are mechanical and physiological reasons. As the uterus grows, the mother's center of gravity shifts forward, and this may affect her sense of balance. She may also have difficulty seeing where she is placing her feet.

At the same time, pregnant women have increasingly unstable joints because of the action of the hormone progesterone. Progesterone loosens the pelvic ligaments, so that the pelvic bones will spread slightly during labor and delivery in order to create more room for the birth—but it has the same loosening effect on all the ligaments and joints of the body.

Other factors that may contribute to instability and accidents during pregnancy are tiredness, slowed reaction time, and preoccupation. A woman may be daydreaming about her baby and absentmindedly miss the edge of a curb and stumble.

Fortunately, most pregnant women have heightened feelings of responsibility and increased vulnerability and so tend to be especially careful. But even when a pregnant woman does fall, it is rare for her baby to be damaged. The fetus is surrounded by the amniotic fluid; the fluid is encased in tough membranes; the membranes are supported by the muscular uterus; and the uterus is in the abdominal cavity, surrounded by the abdominal muscles in the front and the spinal bones and muscles in the back. All in all, it is a very efficient shock-absorbing system. The mother would have to sustain very serious injuries herself before the baby would be harmed.

I was at home one evening when I received an urgent phone call from Bill N., a new neighbor. In an excited voice he said, "I was cleaning an air vent in the living room and my wife fell through the trapdoor to the cellar. She's six months pregnant. I brought her upstairs to the living room couch. She seems all right, but she's seeing double. Can you come over?"

I hurried over to their house, and Bill rushed me into the living room. His wife, Margaret, was lying on the couch with a comforter draped over her. I could see numerous scrapes and bruises, but she was alert and calm.

As I sat beside her, I was thankful for the baby's shock protection. I checked Margaret's breathing and pulse; they were normal. I checked her eyes, and her pupils were normal; by this time she was no longer seeing double. I looked for fractures by feeling her bones to see if they were tender and making sure she could move. Then I put my hand on her abdomen and said, "If you're not bleeding or leaking amniotic fluid from your vagina, and if we feel the baby move, we'll know the baby's probably fine." Margaret said that nothing was leaking, and we waited to feel fetal life. It seemed like a very long wait, but within two or three minutes I felt the baby move. We were all relieved. As I left, I told Margaret to check with her own doctor the next day.

My encounter with my new neighbors serves to illustrate the principles that should be followed for first aid for a pregnant woman after a fall:

- The woman should be kept lying down, comfortable, and warm.
- Be sure she is conscious and breathing normally.
- Check for signs of shock: weakness; pale, clammy skin; rapid, weak pulse; rapid breathing, sometimes shallow or irregular.
- Check for any obvious injuries, such as fractures.
- Check for possible concealed injuries: unusual pain or tenderness, swelling, shock.
- Be sure there is no vaginal bleeding or leaking of amniotic fluid.

- Check for fetal movement. In early pregnancy, medical personnel will listen for the fetal heartbeat.
- Repeat the examination to make sure you haven't missed anything.
- If you note any abnormal signs, get emergency help quickly.
- Have her check with her own doctor promptly, even if there do not seem to be any serious problems.

Most accidents suffered by pregnant women are minor. But major accidents, such as car accidents, can cause major trauma to mother and fetus. Internal injuries and bleeding in the mother can result in shock, which can lead to maternal and fetal death, for example. If the uterus is subjected to extreme tension or pressure, the amniotic sac may break, leading to premature labor. The placenta may become detached from the uterine wall and cause hemorrhaging. A serious interruption in the mother's respiration or heartbeat could adversely affect the fetus's supply of oxygen.

Thus, it is vital to get medical attention immediately after even a minor accident if leaking or bleeding from the vagina, uterine contractions, or anything else unusual is noted—and after *any* major accident.

Not all accidents can be foreseen and prevented, of course. The use of a seat belt, however, can help reduce the chance of serious injury should you be involved in a car accident. A pregnant woman should, when possible, use a shoulder-harness restraint in a car. It is recommended that if she is in a seat that has a lap belt only, she wear it across the pelvic area, not against the abdomen and uterus.

Although a pregnant woman is somewhat more vulnerable to accidents than usual and is likely to be especially concerned about their consequences, she should remember that in most cases her baby is kept safe and sound inside her body.

G.G.P.

# 22. Early Bleeding

Christine N. called me at 8:30 one night. Her voice was filled with urgency and worry as she said, "I'm so frightened! Tom and I had just sat down in the theater when I felt something wet in my pants. When I got to the ladies' room, I saw that my panties were stained red. I've been bleeding! What should I do? Am I having a miscarriage?"

I had examined Christine one week before. She was eager to find out if she and Tom were going to have a baby. Her period was two weeks late then. I was happy to give her the good news: She was six weeks pregnant. Now, at seven weeks, she was very frightened; she felt her pregnancy might be in danger.

A significant proportion of pregnant women may bleed or show some bloody staining in early pregnancy. Most of these pregnancies will continue and will be normal. Statistically, it is probable that bleeding in early pregnancy is *not* a threat to the pregnancy, that the bleeding is incidental and that it will soon pass.

I told Christine that, most likely, her bleeding was not an ominous sign but only the innocuous result of placental implantation in the uterine lining. I explained that the bleeding showed that she needed observation. It was not a good time for the theater; I told her to rest in bed and abstain from intercourse. I asked her to report any heavier bleeding or cramping to me, and told her I would examine her in the morning.

Any bleeding in the first trimester of pregnancy is viewed as a threatened miscarriage until one of the following diagnoses can be made:

- *Implantation bleeding*—probably the cause of the majority of all bleeding
- *Miscarriage*—occurring in about 15 percent of pregnancies
- *Cervical and vaginal infections, polyps, and erosions*—all of which will bleed if irritated by intercourse

- *Ectopic pregnancy*—the rarest, occurring in one out of about 100 pregnancies

A pelvic examination is essential for making the diagnosis. This is perfectly safe and does not harm the fetus. Sometimes, by coincidence, a miscarriage that was destined to occur anyway will happen after the examination. But the examination does not cause the miscarriage.

Christine's examination would show whether the bleeding originated in the uterus itself, the cervix, or the vagina. If a vaginal or cervical infection was present, we could institute treatment to soothe the swollen tissues and stop the bleeding. A cervical polyp is a usually benign growth and needs no treatment; it will usually stop bleeding when the irritation clears up, and it frequently gets pulled off the cervix during the delivery.

When conception occurs outside the uterus (usually within one of the fallopian tubes), it is called an *ectopic pregnancy*. Because it is an abnormal pregnancy, the lining of the uterus is not properly maintained. The lining sheds a bit, and this shows as bleeding. Usually the ectopic pregnancy causes a great deal of pain in the affected tube, and because of internal bleeding from the tube, fainting is common. Pelvic examination shows a growing enlargement in the tube that holds the pregnancy. (This can also be shown with sonography.) Since there is great danger of internal bleeding, an ectopic pregnancy must be removed by surgery without delay.

In the morning, Christine was calmer. "It's just some brown staining now," she reported. She was having no pain or cramps. Her pelvic examination showed no infection or polyps. There was a slight maroon staining coming from the cervix, which was tightly closed; no dilation was taking place. And there was no mass in the region of either fallopian tube.

Most commonly—and it was true in Christine's case— bleeding early in pregnancy represents the phase of active placental implantation. As the placenta forms and expands, fingerlike projections, called *villi*, develop. These placental villi invade the lining of the mother's uterus to establish contact with the mother's blood vessels. This connection must develop so that nutrients will be able to pass from the mother's circulation to the tiny blood vessels in the villi. From here, the blood flows to the fetus via the umbilical cord. As the villi invade the uterine lining, they may cause a break or rupture in a tiny blood vessel of the uterus. Blood may then seep out for a while, until natural healing takes place.

But when bleeding occurs, neither the doctor nor the pregnant woman can tell immediately whether it is the normal implantation bleeding or a signal of serious trouble. With the passage of time, one can see whether the bleeding stops (as it should with implantation bleeding) or progresses (in which case the telltale cramps of miscarriage appear).

Because there is always the possibility that bleeding from the uterus is a sign of impending miscarriage, I ask my patients to rest in bed and abstain from intercourse during those insecure first 24 hours.

One week after Christine's bleeding, I reexamined her to be sure that the uterus was growing properly. The cervix was tightly closed. There was no further bleeding. The uterus was now larger, an eight-week size. We were all relieved that we could resume our optimistic outlook for the future.

G.G.P.

# 23. Ectopic Pregnancy

Melissa came to my office suspecting she was pregnant. Her last normal menstrual period had begun seven weeks before, but she did experience some spotting around the time her next period should have occurred. She was already noticing symptoms that were familiar to her from her first pregnancy—namely, nausea and breast tenderness. In addition, she was experiencing some discomfort in her lower abdomen and did not understand what was causing the pain, since she had not felt so uncomfortable during her previous pregnancy.

We performed a urine test for pregnancy, and it was positive. But when I examined Melissa, I felt a very tender mass next to her uterus. I explained that this was cause for concern and that further testing was necessary to determine if it was a cyst on her ovary or perhaps a tubal pregnancy. I arranged for an ultrasound examination to detect whether or not the pregnancy was indeed in the appropriate place, inside the uterus.

When the ultrasound examination was completed, the scan showed that there was no evidence of a pregnancy within the uterus. A five-centimeter mass was visible to the left of the uterus, as I had noted during the pelvic examination. I suspected that Melissa had an ectopic pregnancy in her left fallopian tube.

Melissa understood that the pregnancy could not thrive inside the fallopian tube and could not continue to grow without causing the tube to rupture. In the interest of preserving Melissa's chances of achieving a normal pregnancy in the future, I recommended immediate hospitalization and surgery to remove the pregnancy before tubal rupture.

All this took place quite quickly. Surgery was performed, the pregnancy was removed, and Melissa was well on the road to recovery. The tube had not ruptured, and it was left in place. Although she understood why the operation was necessary, there were still a lot of questions she needed answered. She wondered why she'd had a tubal pregnancy and if there was a chance she might have another one. She was also concerned about her ability to bear children in the future and wanted to know exactly what had been removed during the surgery.

I explained that the term *ectopic* comes from a Greek root meaning "displaced." In normal pregnancy, the fertilized egg implants in the endometrium, which lines the uterine cavity. If it implants anywhere else, it is called an ectopic pregnancy. Implantation in an ectopic pregnancy most commonly occurs in the fallopian tube, but other sites are possible; implantation on an ovary, in the cervix, or even elsewhere in the abdomen is not unheard of, although certainly not common. Approximately 95 percent of ectopic pregnancies do involve the fallopian tube, though; hence the popular term "tubal pregnancy" for this particular type of ectopic gestation. Although ectopic pregnancies are relatively rare, the incidence seems to be increasing.

A number of factors are known to be associated with an increased risk of tubal pregnancy, including anything that interferes with the structure or function of the fallopian tubes. Previous episodes of pelvic infection, pelvic or abdominal surgery, and endometriosis have all been implicated, as has the presence of an intrauterine device (IUD) for contraception, and even a previous sterilization procedure such as a bilateral tubal ligation. Pelvic infections may damage the tubes so that they do not function normally to transport the fertilized egg. Even though the failure rate (meaning pregnancies) for tubal ligation is still quite low (fewer than one to four per 1,000 procedures), 5 to 10 percent of women who have an ectopic pregnancy have had a tubal ligation.

Whenever a woman complains of having missed a period or of having an abnormal period and has the usual symptoms of early pregnancy plus lower abdominal pain or discomfort, physicians become concerned about the possibility of an ectopic pregnancy. Problems arise in making the correct diagnosis, however, since a number of conditions may cause similar symptoms. A ruptured or unruptured ovarian cyst, pelvic infection, appendicitis, or urinary tract infection may be confused with an ectopic pregnancy.

A pregnancy test is helpful in making the diagnosis, but a urine test may be negative. This is because in an ectopic pregnancy, the placenta generally secretes less human chorionic gonadotrophin (the hormone indicating pregnancy in tests) than does the placenta of a normal pregnancy of the same gestational age within the uterus. If a physician strongly suspects an ectopic pregnancy, a more sensitive blood test can be performed. An ultrasound examination may be helpful in localizing the site of a pregnancy, either through visualization of a gestational sac within the uterus itself or by revealing a mass outside the uterus, in the area of the fallopian tube, for example.

There is also a surgical procedure, *diagnostic laparoscopy,* that enables a physician to see the pelvic organs using an instrument called a *laparoscope*. (It is about the diameter of my little finger and is something like a telescope with lenses.) This procedure can be used to confirm the presence of a cyst or to help diagnose a tubal pregnancy. Although general anesthesia is usually used for this operation, the surgical incision is a small one. If the laparoscopy reveals a cyst, further surgery may not be necessary, but if there is a tubal pregnancy, surgery will be required to remove it.

The type of surgery performed depends to some extent on whether the tube has ruptured. The abdominal pain associated with a tubal pregnancy is usually relatively mild if the tube has not ruptured. The symptoms of a ruptured tubal pregnancy are much more dramatic and may include sudden, severe pain, fainting, and a significant drop in blood pressure and hematocrit (the percentage of red blood cells in the whole blood by volume) as a result of bleeding into the abdomen from the ruptured tube. A ruptured ectopic pregnancy is indeed a surgical emergency. It is, of course, preferable if the diagnosis can be made prior to the rupture, if at all possible.

In the past, the standard type of surgery for a tubal ectopic pregnancy, whether ruptured or unruptured, was the removal of the entire fallopian tube. While this may still be necessary, particularly if it has ruptured, many gynecologists now consider the possibility of conserving the fallopian tube, either by removing the pregnancy through the end of the tube or by making a small incision in one side of the tube and removing just the pregnancy tissue, not the entire tube. Although this is certainly not possible in every case, leaving the organ in place allows for the possibility of spontaneous healing of the tube or further surgery at some point in the future to reconstruct it.

In cases of tubal pregnancy, the earlier the diagnosis, the better. Early detection increases the chances that future childbearing will be possible, because it enables a physician to take the proper measures to remove the pregnancy before the fallopian tube ruptures. Since women who have had one ectopic pregnancy have an increased chance of having another, I would advise these women, especially, to seek medical care as soon as possible if they suspect they are pregnant.

P.A.H.

# 24. Miscarriage

Nancy W. called my office in tears. I had seen her the previous week for her first prenatal visit and the diagnosis of a much-wanted pregnancy. At that time, all had appeared to be normal. Her uterus was an appropriate size for an eight-week pregnancy, and she was experiencing only mild symptoms of nausea and breast tenderness. Today, however, she told me that she was having heavy bleeding and cramping. I arranged to meet her in the emergency room of the hospital.

After a brief pelvic examination, it was apparent that Nancy was having a miscarriage. I explained to Nancy and her husband, Bill, that unfortunately the pregnancy could not continue normally and that there was nothing more that could be done to prevent a miscarriage. I further explained that a *uterine curettage*—a medical procedure to empty the uterus of its contents—would be necessary to make sure no pregnancy tissue remained. If any tissue was left in the uterus, the bleeding would continue.

Nancy and Bill had a few moments together to comfort each other and absorb the impact of the pregnancy loss while preparations for the curettage were being made. Afterward we again discussed the situation. I told Nancy to take it easy for a few days in order to allow herself to recover physically from the miscarriage. I also explained that she and her husband should be prepared to experience feelings of sadness and grief at the loss of their baby.

Nancy was puzzled by the fact that she had had a miscarriage and expressed concern that it might have been due to her exercise classes. I reassured her that nothing she had done had caused it and that she should not feel guilty. More than half of all early miscarriages (within the first trimester) are a result of chromosomal or genetic abnormalities that prevent normal development of the fetus. Most of these abnormalities occur at random, and her chances of having a normal subsequent pregnancy were good.

Reassured, Nancy was eager to try again and wanted to know how long it would be before she could become pregnant.

I recommended she wait two or three months, for a number of reasons. First of all, a woman needs time to recover physically, particularly from the bleeding experienced during a miscarriage. In addition, a two- or three-month wait will give her body time to reestablish a normal cycle of ovulation and menstruation. It will also allow her time to adjust psychologically and resolve her feelings of grief over the loss of her baby. I scheduled Nancy for an appointment in two weeks, and she went home to rest.

When Nancy returned for her checkup, she said she had felt sad, but physically she was fine and had resumed her normal activities. She had been able to share her feelings with her mother, who had also suffered a miscarriage before having four healthy children, and was optimistically looking toward the future.

Five months later, Nancy was again pregnant. She did not announce her pregnancy to friends and acquaintances quite as early as she had the first time. By the middle of the second trimester, when she began to wear maternity clothes, she was feeling relieved at having made it through the first trimester without difficulties or problems, and I reassured her that the chances were very good that the pregnancy would continue normally. Later that year, Nancy and Bill were delighted at the birth of a healthy son.

An estimated 15 to 20 percent of all pregnancies end in miscarriage—or, in medical terms, *spontaneous abortion*—early in the pregnancy. Some of these pregnancies are not even recognized by a woman or her physician, and bleeding that occurs only slightly late may be interpreted as a normal menstrual period rather than a very early miscarriage. The increasing use of sensitive blood tests for pregnancy may lead to the recognition of still more miscarriages.

Most pregnancy losses do take place within the first twelve to thirteen weeks of pregnancy. Death of the embryo or fetus nearly always occurs prior to the onset of bleeding. Studies indicate that most early miscarriages are associated with abnormal development or chromosomal abnormalities of the fetus, or sometimes abnormalities of the placenta. In a sense, these pregnancies are destined to miscarry. Other potential causes of early pregnancy loss include reproductive-tract infections (in rare instances), chronic illnesses, or hormonal imbalances.

Some women do have more than one miscarriage. Repeated miscarriages may occur by chance, or there may be a physiological reason for them. If a woman has two or three consecutive miscarriages, most physicians will recommend further testing.

Pregnancy loss beyond the first trimester may result from uterine abnormalities, and if a woman has a history of pregnancy loss, her physician will likely recommend testing, although a specific cause may not be found. If the cause is determined, however, the condition can sometimes be rectified. For example, some women do not carry their pregnancies to term because their cervix dilates when the pregnancy reaches a certain stage, usually during the second or early third trimester. This condition, known as *incompetent cervix*, can often be surgically remedied.

Sometimes women fear they are going to miscarry when they experience bleeding during pregnancy, and the term *threatened miscarriage* is indeed used to describe bleeding during the first half of pregnancy. However, one out of every four or five women have some bleeding in early pregnancy, and most early pregnancies accompanied by a small amount of vaginal bleeding continue normally and result in healthy babies. Most physicians do recommend an examination to determine other possible causes for the bleeding, but if it is not associated with cramping and if it is not severe, they will usually advise their patients to rest and to abstain from sexual intercourse until the bleeding stops.

An ultrasound examination to determine other possible causes may also be helpful in predicting the outcome of a pregnancy complicated by early bleeding. Often, though, the only possible recommendation is that time will determine whether the pregnancy will continue or a miscarriage will occur. Unfortunately, the waiting period is often very difficult for the woman and her partner because of the uncertainty of the situation.

There is often little that can be done to prevent miscarriage. It is deemed inevitable once the membranes have ruptured and the cervix is dilated, or if some of the pregnancy tissue has been expelled.

A miscarriage may be a frightening event for any woman. Accurate information about the frequency of miscarriages, the possible causes, the chances for normal future pregnancies, and the normalcy of a reaction of grief may help to ease the physical and emotional pain.

P.A.H.

# 25. Urinary Infection

Last year, a very anxious couple came to my office for the first time to confirm a feared pregnancy. The patient, Joanne W., was 32 years old and pregnant for the third time. Her husband, Bob, was a successful attorney and a devoted husband. They requested an abortion rather than risk a repeat of the *pyelonephritis* (infection of the kidneys) that had complicated Joanne's previous pregnancies.

Joanne's first pregnancy had progressed normally until the middle of her eighth month. At that time she noted urinary burning, back pain, and a temperature of 100° F. Her obstetrician prescribed oral antibiotics and sent her home to rest in bed. That night, her fever spiked to 104, and she had a shaking chill. Simultaneously, she went into premature labor, and she soon delivered a premature girl weighing 2,000 grams (less than four and a half pounds). After intensive care for respiratory distress syndrome (a lung problem that affects prematures), the infant did well. And Joanne responded quickly to antibiotics. She was discharged from the hospital on her fifth postpartum day.

At 28 weeks of her second pregnancy, Joanne again complained of urinary burning, back pain, and low-grade fever. She was hospitalized immediately that time, and she was treated with intravenous antibiotics. Her response was rapid, and her temperature quickly returned to normal. Her urinary burning and back pain improved but, because of her previous experience, she was kept hospitalized for three months. She was given repeat courses of antibiotics. She went into labor at 38 weeks, two weeks before her due date, and she delivered a normal, full-term girl.

The apprehension of this couple was understandable. Joanne showed me her *intravenous pyelogram* (a kidney X ray that shows the kidneys and the ureters, the tubes that lead urine from the kidneys to the bladder), which had been taken three days after her second delivery. It showed characteristic changes of the ureter that occur in pregnancy: dilation and slight elongation. The kidneys were normal. Another X ray, taken six months after the delivery, was normal; the changes associated with pregnancy were gone.

I told the couple that I believed that by applying current knowledge of the urinary tract in pregnancy and, by heeding the warnings of Joanne's history of pyelonephritis, we would have a good chance of avoiding the complication during this pregnancy. Fortunately, she and Bob bravely chose to proceed with the pregnancy.

Acute (sudden-onset) pyelonephritis is one of the most common complications of pregnancy. In over 90 percent of the cases, the causative organism is a bacterium called *Escherichia coli*, referred to as *E. coli* for short. Acute pyelonephritis must be considered an obstetric emergency requiring immediate hospitalization and treatment with intravenous antibiotics. The clinical picture of symptoms and signs can change drastically within one or two hours, and the resultant high fever and the release of poisonlike toxins by the *E. coli* can cause miscarriage or premature labor.

Studies have shown that as many as 5 percent of pregnant women with no symptoms of urinary illness are carriers of bacteria in their urine. In medical terms, this is called *asymptomatic bacteriuria*. Pyelonephritis in pregnancy occurs more often in patients with asymptomatic bacteriuria, and it has been shown that treatment of women who have asymptomatic bacteriuria *does* prevent the ensuing pyelonephritis from developing.

As long ago as 1936, gynecologists H. F. Traut and C. M.

McLane had published their studies of the physiological changes in the ureter associated with pregnancy in the journal *Surgery, Gynecology and Obstetrics*. Traut and McLane showed that there is a progressive loss of the tone of the ureter wall during pregnancy, with resultant dilation of the ureter. This widening of the urinary tract is associated with slowing of the downward urine flow, which provides opportunity for bacteria of the urinary bladder to travel up to the kidneys.

I could get some measure of the slowing of the flow of urine down to Joanne's ureters by studying her two intravenous pyelograms. I had one that was normal and another, taken three days after childbirth, still showing the changes of pregnancy. Using the intravenous pyelogram taken six months later, Joanne's normal, nonpregnant ureter was found to average 0.6 centimeters in diameter (about a quarter of an inch), but in pregnancy, that diameter doubled to an average 1.2 centimeters, or about half an inch. Application of the geometry of areas showed that Joanne would have to drink four times as much liquid during pregnancy to get her urine to flow down her pregnant ureters as fast as it flowed down when she was not pregnant.

Joanne had urine cultures done every four weeks and a urinalysis every two weeks. At four and a half months of pregnancy, a urinalysis showed many bacteria, and a urine culture showed large amounts of *E. coli*. But Joanne still had no symptoms.

She was started on an antibiotic, and I explained that she must increase her fluid intake to four liters (about four quarts) a day. I explained the problem of urinary stasis, or slowing, and I insisted that she keep records of fluid intake daily in order to ensure an adequate urinary outflow. Within 48 hours, her urine cultures were sterile. She was kept on a prophylactic (preventive) dose of antibiotic throughout the pregnancy. The urine remained sterile and voluminous.

At 39 weeks, Joanne delivered her third daughter. And she had lost no time from family responsibilities.

Because the normal rigors of childbirth cause swelling of the bladder and the *urethra* (the channel through which urine flows out of the bladder), Joanne was advised to continue her antibacterial drug and her high fluid intake. *Involution* (the returning to normal) of the urinary tract usually takes four to six weeks, so that regimen continued until then.

The principles guiding Joanne's treatment apply to all pregnant women. Pregnancy causes a loss in muscle tone of the ureters, so that the flow of urine down to the bladder is slowed. Because of this there is a greater chance that bacteria, which are often present in the bladder without symptoms, can make their way up toward the kidneys. In addition, the pregnant woman uses up more fluid because of the formation of amniotic fluid and the increase in circulating-blood volume; she also uses fluid in increased sweating and increased water metabolism due to the action of hormones of pregnancy.

When you are pregnant, you should increase your fluid intake to four quarts or more each day. This will almost eliminate your chance of having a urinary infection.

G.G.P.

# 26. Iron-Deficiency Anemia

You have probably seen television commercials or newspaper and magazine advertisements that emphasize the importance of iron in a woman's diet. The condition known as *iron-deficiency anemia*, the "iron-poor blood" syndrome that results when the supply of iron does not meet the body's requirements, is one of the most common complications of pregnancy. It is, however, also one of the most treatable.

Iron is essential for the manufacture of new blood cells and also plays a part in the blood's transportation of oxygen throughout the body. A major component of blood is a clear, slightly yellowish fluid called *plasma*. Many different substances, including white and red blood cells, are suspended in this fluid. *Hemoglobin* is the molecule within the red blood cells that gives the cells their red color, and iron is a key element in this molecule.

These cells carry oxygen to various tissues throughout the body and also carry off the cells' waste product, carbon dioxide. If sufficient iron is not available from iron stores in food, or if iron is not absorbed efficiently through the digestive tract, iron deficiency occurs. The amount of hemoglobin in the red blood cells decreases, and the oxygen available to the cells in the body tissues diminishes. When the amount of hemoglobin falls below a certain level, the condition is known as *anemia*.

The definition of anemia is based on measurements of the blood hemoglobin or hematocrit. The hemoglobin content of blood is expressed in grams per 100 cubic centimeters (cc). The *hematocrit* is expressed as a percentage of red blood cells in the whole blood by volume. Hematocrit levels in women normally range from over 30 percent to the low forties.

Hemoglobin and hematocrit concentrations of men and women are different, as are the "normal" concentrations of pregnant and nonpregnant women. The nonpregnant woman is considered to be anemic if her hemoglobin concentration is less than 12 grams per 100 cc. Anemia during pregnancy or the immediate postpartum period is defined by a hemoglobin concentration of less than 10 grams per 100 cc. This corresponds to a hematocrit of less than 30 percent.

Since the volume of blood increases during pregnancy, more iron is needed to make new red blood cells for both the mother and the developing baby. During the course of pregnancy, the blood plasma volume increases by 50 percent, while the mass of red blood cells increases by only 25 percent. Since the volume of red blood cells does not increase as much as the fluid (plasma) in which the cells are suspended, the hematocrit will normally decrease somewhat during pregnancy, reaching the lowest point around the thirtieth week.

Although the volume of blood does not increase at as rapid a rate during the last trimester of pregnancy, the need for iron remains high, because iron is being transported from the mother to the fetus across the placenta. The fetus is very efficient at obtaining the amount of iron it needs to build its blood, and babies are not born with iron-deficiency anemia, even if their mothers are severely anemic. But unless the difference between the amount of iron the mother has stored and the iron requirements of pregnancy is made up by iron in the diet, a pregnant woman will develop iron-deficiency anemia.

Normally, when the body's supply of iron is adequate to supply its needs, excess iron is stored in the bone marrow. Because nonpregnant women have a monthly drain (the menstrual period) on their iron stores, most women have very small reserves of iron, and many have no iron stored. Since the iron requirements of pregnancy usually considerably exceed the iron stores of even healthy women, it is important to incorporate foods rich in iron into the daily diet.

The best sources of iron are liver (chicken livers included) and lean red meats. Iron-enriched cereals are also good sources, as are dark leafy greens, chicken, and fish. Raisins, prunes, other dried fruits, and blackstrap molasses also contain iron; dried beans and pasta do also, though not as much.

In addition, the American College of Obstetricians and Gynecologists recommends that with rare exception, every pregnant woman receive iron supplements. I know no one likes to take pills. It is difficult to remember to take a pill on a daily basis, particularly if one is feeling well and not taking medication to "get well." But it is extremely important that pregnant women actually take the iron pills prescribed.

Karen B. is a case in point. She came to see me for the first prenatal visit when she was eight weeks pregnant. Her examination confirmed that all was going well with the pregnancy. However, when I reviewed the lab tests, I found that her hematocrit was 34 percent. Although she was not considered truly anemic—since her hematocrit was above 30 percent—her body was going to require additional iron to produce more red blood cells for both her and her developing baby. She told me that her periods had been heavy just before her pregnancy, so her iron stores were probably quite low. I emphasized that an iron supplement would be necessary.

At the next visit, I asked Karen if she had been taking her iron. She hesitated and finally admitted that it was "just hard to remember." I suggested that she leave the bottle of iron supplements next to the box of cereal so that she would be reminded to take the iron each morning. When I repeated the blood test at a later prenatal visit, her hematocrit was improved. Karen continued her iron supplements and did not become anemic during her pregnancy.

Most prenatal vitamin supplements contain some iron, and many doctors prescribe additional iron supplements, which come in a variety of forms: capsules, timed-release capsules, tablets, and liquid preparations. Absorption of iron is slowed by some foods, including milk and eggs, as well as by some antacids. Ideally, iron should be taken on an empty stomach. However, some women who take iron experience discomfort, such as intestinal cramping, nausea, constipation, or diarrhea. These symptoms can be minimized somewhat by taking the iron with small amounts of food or by switching to a timed-release or coated capsule.

If constipation becomes a problem, drinking more fluids, eating fiber-rich foods, and getting more exercise may be helpful. If the problem persists, a stool softener can be prescribed. It is also important to note that when a woman takes iron supplements, her stools will likely appear very dark brown or black. This is to be expected and is not a cause for alarm. If a woman is indeed intolerant of oral iron, injections may be given. Stopping the iron is not the solution.

Iron supplements should be continued for three to six months after the delivery of the baby. The loss of blood during delivery further depletes a woman's iron supply, and it is necessary to build up an adequate iron reserve.

*Warning*: I would like to add one final word of caution. A small child can easily consume a fatal dose of iron supplements. Women who have small children at home should keep these supplements in a child-proof bottle, out of the reach of children.

P.A.H.

# 27. Varicose Veins and Hemorrhoids

Advances in medical care have served to improve today's pregnancy in numerous ways. Yet many of the daily physical inconveniences of pregnancy are essentially unchanged from previous generations. For example, normal physiological changes in pregnancy can cause some susceptible women to develop varicose veins or hemorrhoids.

*Varicose veins* are veins that are abnormally dilated and unusually knotted. They may be painful as well as unsightly. It is a condition that usually affects the superficial veins in the legs; it does not often affect deep veins, since they are surrounded by muscles that keep them compressed.

*Hemorrhoids* are anal veins that have become varicose; they are swollen and often painful or itchy.

Understanding the physiology of the venous system and its changes during pregnancy will help you see that although much of the propensity to get varicose veins and hemorrhoids is out of your control, you can help to minimize their impact.

When you have your blood pressure taken, the pressure of the blood within your *arteries*—the blood vessels that conduct blood away from the heart—is being measured. There is also pressure within the *veins*—the vessels returning blood to the heart—but it is usually much lower than in the arteries. When you are lying down, the venous pressure is about one-tenth the arterial pressure. But the pressure within the leg veins—those most likely to become varicose—is related to the upright distance from the calf of the leg to the heart. So when you are standing, this pressure is substantially increased, and the veins, which have less strong walls than the arteries, may dilate.

Moreover, the blood in the legs must travel against gravity to return to the heart. There is a system of one-way valves within the veins, enabling the blood to flow only toward the heart. If many of these valves are missing or defective—a condition that may be hereditary—a person is more likely to get varicose veins: The blood may drop back down and pool in the system, swelling the veins.

When a woman is pregnant, there are several factors that may increase her chances of developing varicose veins.

The first is increased blood volume. During pregnancy, the mother's blood volume increases by about 45 percent, reaching its maximum at the end of the seventh month. The extra pints of blood are necessary in order to nourish the growing uterus and its contents, the placenta and the baby. All the veins in the body dilate to help accommodate the extra blood, and pregnant women may notice that even the veins on the backs of the hands become swollen.

This general enlargement of the veins may prevent normal venous valves from closing entirely, and for those women with missing or defective valves, even more blood will fall back and swell the leg veins, particularly when they are standing. The veins around the anus may also expand and bulge out, appearing under the skin as hemorrhoids.

Second, the increased amount of the hormone progesterone present during pregnancy may add to the tendency of the veins to enlarge because it relaxes all smooth muscle, including blood vessel walls.

The growing uterus also contributes to increasing venous pressure. As it grows, it presses on the pelvic veins that are returning blood to the heart. This increases the resistance to flow, in turn increasing the pressure within the veins of the legs and the anus.

How can you apply this information to helping yourself?

First, by lying down, you eliminate the falling back of the blood down the veins and thus reduce the effects of venous pressure. It is neither practical nor healthy to spend an entire pregnancy lying down, but you can minimize your standing whenever possible. Sit instead of standing when you can, and prop your legs up on a chair or stool in order to reduce the pressure further.

You can encourage the blood to return to the heart by exercise such as walking; moving the leg muscles will help pump the blood upward.

You can help the relatively inelastic, thin-walled veins resist dilation by wearing support stockings. Since the blood volume begins to increase with the start of pregnancy, it is a good habit to begin to wear support panty hose as soon as you suspect that you are pregnant.

And if you see that you are developing varicose veins and hemorrhoids, you can wear a maternity girdle, which will lift up the uterus and diminish the pressure against the pelvic veins.

Pregnant women are prone to constipation because of uterine pressure on the rectum and the relaxant effect of progesterone on the bowels. The bulky presence of the constipated fecal material and the pushing necessary to expel it will increase the pressure on the veins in the pelvis and this, too, can encourage hemorrhoids. Pregnant women should seek and follow their doctors' advice for avoiding or relieving constipation.

It must be added that adequate water intake is essential for the increased metabolic requirements of pregnancy. If you are not drinking enough water, your system will extract it from the intestines, leaving you with a dry, firm—constipating—stool. I recommend that a pregnant woman worried by the possibility of hemorrhoids drink twelve glasses (three quarts) of water a day.

G.G.P.

# 28. Gestational Diabetes

Ann, age 36, was pregnant with her first child. She was excited but also a little anxious about the possible complications of pregnancy. In reviewing her family history for medical problems, she noted that her mother's mother and aunt had had diabetes. "I have heard that pregnant women can develop diabetes," she said. "Should I cut out sugar to prevent my getting it?"

Her question warranted a detailed explanation. The term *diabetes* refers to several disorders, each involving problems in the way the body handles sugar (glucose). If these problems begin or are first recognized during pregnancy, the disease is called *gestational* (pregnancy-related) *diabetes*. Women like Ann, who have a family history of diabetes, do have an increased chance of developing it when they are pregnant. Ann's age was also a predisposing factor. I recommended that we do a relatively simple screening test to check for abnormal blood-glucose levels. If the glucose level was high, another test would be necessary to confirm the problem.

Women with gestational diabetes can usually control their blood sugar through diet. Eliminating sugar from the diet will not prevent gestational diabetes, nor is it necessary to do so if the condition develops. I further explained to Ann that it was incorrect for her to assume that she would develop diabetes just because her grandmother had the disorder. It was necessary to see the test results first. Eventually, tests confirmed that her blood-sugar levels were normal.

There are actually three main types of diabetes mellitus (its full technical name): Type I, or insulin-dependent diabetes, which commonly (although not always) begins in childhood and is sometimes called *juvenile diabetes;* Type II, or non-insulin-dependent diabetes, sometimes called *maturity-onset diabetes*, which is more common in overweight adults; and *gestational diabetes*, which occurs during pregnancy and then usually goes away after delivery. All three types are associated with elevated levels of glucose in the blood. Glucose is a simple sugar that the body's cells use for fuel. Insulin, produced by the pancreas, is required for glucose to enter the cells. Although insulin levels in each of the types of diabetes may vary, the body's metabolism or ability to use glucose is altered in all three. Hence, the term *impaired glucose tolerance during pregnancy,* which some physicians prefer to *gestational diabetes*. The general term *diabetes* also has some associations that may not be true for pregnancy-related glucose intolerance.

During pregnancy, the levels of estrogen, progesterone, cortisol, and placental hormones increase. Hormones affect the way the mother's body uses the glucose found in the food she eats. In a normal pregnancy, the hormonal changes result in blood-glucose levels that are slightly higher after eating and slightly lower when food intake has been limited (such as first thing in the morning) than when a woman is not pregnant.

A small percentage of pregnant women (fewer than 3 percent) develop a transitory disturbance in glucose tolerance, resulting in elevated levels of blood sugar. If it is unrecognized or untreated, babies born to these mothers are more likely to have problems during the latter part of pregnancy, during labor, or shortly after birth. Undiagnosed gestational diabetes may also occasionally be a cause of otherwise unexplained stillbirth. In an effort to prevent these problems, screening tests have been developed.

Physicians often use a specific set of criteria to decide which women have a higher statistical risk of developing gestational diabetes. They will test blood-glucose levels of pregnant women who have sugar in their urine (*glycosuria*); who have previously delivered a very large baby; who have had pregnancy losses; who are significantly overweight; who have a family history of diabetes; and/or who are older than 25 or 30. In some studies of women with gestational diabetes, the mother's age was found to be the most significant risk factor. Some physicians will test the blood-glucose levels of *all* their pregnant patients.

A *glucose-challenge test* is generally used for screening purposes. It entails drinking a concentrated glucose solution, usually given as a cola-flavored drink, and then testing a blood sample for glucose one hour later. Normal values have been established, but if the glucose level registers higher, it does not necessarily mean that the woman has gestational diabetes. If blood glucose is normal but the woman has a number of risk factors, an obstetrician may recommend a repeat screening test around the twenty-eighth week of pregnancy.

If the screening test shows higher-than-normal blood-sugar levels, a *glucose-tolerance test* will be performed. This time, twice as much glucose is given. Blood is taken and tested four times—the first time after an overnight fast, and then at one, two, and three hours after the test dose of glucose. If two of the four values are too high, the diagnosis of impaired glucose tolerance during pregnancy, or gestational diabetes, is made.

The treatment for gestational diabetes is individualized, but it usually involves dietary modifications in order to allow appropriate but not excessive weight gain. Suggestions usually include decreased fat intake, modified carbohydrate intake emphasizing more complex carbohydrates, and a decrease in concentrated glucose from sweets. Alcohol intake should be eliminated.

Blood-glucose levels are then monitored throughout the pregnancy. If a woman with impaired glucose tolerance is conscientiously following her diet, and her weight gain is appropriate but the glucose levels remain too high, additional treatment in the form of insulin injections may be necessary.

Another indicator of blood-glucose levels is hemoglobin $A_{1C}$. Glucose is bound to some of the hemoglobin molecules, and since this molecule remains intact for a long time, the overall levels of blood glucose for the previous four to six weeks are reflected in the levels of hemoglobin $A_{1C}$. Some physicians will periodically measure this blood substance, as well.

Although pregnancy for most gestational diabetics proceeds normally, women with the condition are still considered in the moderately high-risk category. Various methods of monitoring the mother's and baby's health may be used during the pregnancy. If no other obstetrical problems develop, the onset of labor is usually awaited. If, however, spontaneous labor does not begin by the fortieth week, many obstetricians will consider inducing labor, or they may monitor the baby's health through fetal-activity testing or contraction stress tests. In order to avoid potential problems, the pregnancy is usually not allowed to go "postterm." Whether labor is spontaneous or induced, electronic fetal monitoring is necessary. Because the babies in these instances may be large, they are more likely to experience problems related to their size at birth, and a cesarean delivery may be necessary. After birth, the baby is observed closely to detect any transient problems in regulating the infant's own blood sugar.

With appropriate attention to diet and good prenatal care, most mothers with gestational diabetes will deliver normal, healthy babies. The problem often resolves after delivery, although another glucose-tolerance test should be performed six to twelve weeks postpartum. For some women, a mildly impaired glucose tolerance will persist, and a woman with a history of gestational diabetes does have a greater chance of developing overt diabetes, particularly if she is overweight. It is especially important, therefore, that such women attain and maintain recommended weight after delivery.

P.A.H.

# 29. Preeclampsia

Terry's first baby was due the next week. So far, her pregnancy had progressed normally, but as I read over her prenatal chart on my way to the examining room, I was alarmed by some new developments: Her blood pressure was up, and her urine check indicated the presence of protein. She had also gained four pounds since the previous week.

When I asked her how she felt, her only complaint was that her ankles had become more swollen and she was finding it difficult to remove her rings. She seemed surprised when I expressed concern. "But I really feel fine," she protested. I explained that she had developed a condition known as *preeclampsia* and that if it progressed, both she and the baby would be in great danger. I recommended she be hospitalized that afternoon.

Preeclampsia is a mysterious disease. It is a problem that complicates 5 to 7 percent of pregnancies in the United States. It occurs in the latter months of pregnancy and affects primarily young, healthy women who are pregnant for the first time. Most women with preeclampsia feel perfectly well; yet, if left untreated, mothers and babies can die from the condition.

Medical scientists are searching for the cause of preeclampsia, and a multitude of theories have been proposed. Still, the cause remains obscure. The problem does, however, resolve quickly after delivery, and doctors have made progress in detecting and treating the disease and in preventing the severe problems associated with it.

The term *preeclampsia* refers to a condition signaled by

several symptoms: *hypertension*, elevated blood pressure; *edema*, tissue swelling or fluid retention; and/or *proteinuria*, the presence of protein in the urine. The condition is sometimes referred to as *toxemia of pregnancy*, but *toxemia* is a poor term, since it implies that the disease is caused by a toxin or poison in the mother's blood, and no such toxin has been identified. If the disease progresses and is left untreated, it may develop into a more serious form, *eclampsia*, which is characterized by seizures or convulsions.

Although eclampsia can occur suddenly and without warning, today, it is primarily a disease of neglect. Either a woman does not understand the importance of regular prenatal visits, or (occasionally) a physician will fail to detect the early symptoms of preeclampsia. Frequent doctor visits (every two weeks) during the last trimester of pregnancy and weekly visits during the last month are important, so that the early signs of preeclampsia can be detected.

Blood-pressure monitoring is an integral part of prenatal care. Blood-pressure measurements consist of two numbers: the higher number (*systolic blood pressure*) represents the pressure in the blood vessels when the heart contracts; the lower number (*diastolic blood pressure*) is the pressure when the heart relaxes between beats. A normal reading during pregnancy would be written as 110/70, for example. In preeclampsia, blood pressure increases; the systolic blood pressure rises to over 140 or the diastolic pressure to greater than 90.

Another warning signal of preeclampsia is edema. Most pregnant women experience some fluid retention, and it is usually not a cause for concern. In preeclampsia, the edema is often generalized; swelling or puffiness is evident not only in the legs and ankles but also in the hands and face. Sudden and excessive weight gain (four pounds or more in one week), especially during the last month of pregnancy, may be cause for alarm, since this degree of weight increase nearly always reflects fluid retention. If it is accompanied by an elevation in blood pressure and the presence of urinary protein, preeclampsia should be strongly suspected.

Protein in the urine in greater than trace amounts, incidentally, is abnormal, but not necessarily indicative of preeclampsia. A bladder or kidney infection can sometimes result in proteinuria. It is important, however, to determine the cause of the problem.

When a doctor detects only a mild increase in blood pressure or a greater than average amount of edema, bed rest (lying on the side with legs and feet elevated) at home may be recommended. It's particularly important to take it easy and to avoid activities that require long periods of standing and walking. If a pregnant woman is working outside her home, this is the time to stop working, both for her own sake and for the health of her unborn baby. Frequent blood-pressure and urine checks will be necessary, but sometimes the condition will require no further treatment. Development of severe headaches, visual changes, or abdominal pain warrants a call to the doctor.

If edema increases or blood pressure elevates in spite of home bed rest, or if proteinuria increases, hospitalization is required. Although a woman may feel fine, it is best that she be in a setting where her health and the baby's can be closely monitored. If her condition were to worsen, with no treatment at hand, she might suffer a stroke; heart, liver, or kidney failure; or seizures. Any of these would endanger both her and her unborn child.

The only real *cure* for preeclampsia is delivery of the baby. Since the disease occurs primarily at or near term, a physician may choose to wait until the spontaneous onset of labor to deliver the child. If blood pressure, edema, or proteinuria increases, however, labor may have to be induced.

The decision to induce labor can be difficult, especially if severe preeclampsia develops during the period from 28 to 36 weeks, when the baby may be at risk for problems associated with prematurity. The recommendation for inducing labor is based on a careful assessment and balancing of the risks to the mother and baby with the progression of preeclampsia, and the need for the pregnancy to continue to allow the baby to grow and mature.

In Terry's case, her blood pressure continued to be elevated after she had been hospitalized, and protein was found in her urine. Since she was only one week from her due date, I felt it was preferable for her baby to be delivered sooner rather than later and recommended inducing labor first thing in the morning. Terry ageed and spent the evening with her husband reviewing what they had learned in their prepared-childbirth classes.

At 8:00 A.M., Terry received intravenous oxytocin to start labor. When oxytocin is given in careful dosage increments, a normal labor pattern can be simulated. In two hours, Terry was having strong, regular contractions. Her blood pressure increased somewhat during labor, and she was given magnesium sulfate, a standard drug used to prevent the convulsions associated with eclampsia. This medication has little or no effect on the baby and can be lifesaving for the mother.

The rest of Terry's labor progressed normally, and her vigorous and healthy son, Gregory, was born at 4:20 P.M. Terry received intravenous magnesium sulfate for several hours after delivery, but by the next day she was back in her room, holding and nursing her baby. Her blood pressure had returned to normal, and she was losing through urination the excess fluid she had been retaining. She and her baby went home on the third day after delivery, and her blood pressure has been normal ever since.

Terry's was a typical case. Fortunately, after delivery, the signs of preeclampsia usually disappear rapidly. There is very little risk that the mother will continue to have high blood pressure or that the problem will recur with subsequent pregnancies. Most mothers who have had preeclampsia return home healthy and bring home healthy babies—which is, after all, the goal of good prenatal care.

P.A.H.

# 30. The "Incompetent" Cervix

In medicine, as in life in general, there may be many paths that lead to the same end point. Most normal life situations do not cause nervousness or anxiety, and the choices are generally easy. You might argue over whether to take one highway or another on a trip, but you don't get terribly upset if one route takes a little longer or hits more red lights. This is because *getting there* is what matters.

In medicine, there are often many equally valid treatments for the same problem. Which treatment should be followed is up to the patient. To help her make a clear and informed decision, the patient should discuss the management of the condition with her doctor, asking: What are all the methods of treatment for this condition? What are the advantages and disadvantages, and the statistics of success and failure—and how do these relate to my medical history?

The following story illustrates how two patients with the same condition made different choices, and yet each solved her problem.

One week recently, I delivered the babies of two mothers named Patricia. The women both had similar problems in maintaining their pregnancies. Although their pregnancies were managed differently, each Patricia reached her goal of having a healthy child, and each left the hospital happy and satisfied.

Patricia W. was 32 and contemplating her third pregnancy. Her first baby had been born very prematurely, at 28 weeks. The tiny boy lived only three days and died from lung complications of prematurity.

When she was pregnant for the second time, she was watched carefully for *cervical incompetence,* a condition in which the cervix, or mouth of the uterus, lacks the necessary muscular strength to resist the pressure of pregnancy. As the fetus grows, the downward pressure causes the cervix to efface, or thin out. Next, the cervix dilates. This happens painlessly. Usually the mother notices nothing unusual until the baby actually starts to move down the birth passage. Such babies are usually born prematurely, often at home or on the way to the hospital. Even when the mother is in the hospital, the birth is so fast that the doctor or midwife may not get there in time.

I examined Patricia W. every week during her second pregnancy. Sure enough, her cervix began to efface and to dilate at the end of the sixth month of pregnancy. Patricia's treatment was to stay home in bed for the next two months. Her feet were elevated to reduce the pressure against the cervix. She was allowed up only briefly to go to the bathroom.

With reduced pressure against the cervix, extreme prematurity was prevented. The baby was born at the end of the eighth month. Nila, a lovely, healthy girl, weighed six pounds.

Pat O. was also 32 years old, and she, too, was contemplating her third pregnancy. Her first baby had also been born prematurely, at 26 weeks, and had lived for only two weeks.

When Pat O. was pregnant for the second time, she, too, was watched carefully for cervical incompetence. She had weekly examinations. At 22 weeks, her cervix was not effaced and was closed. Two days later, without any prior warning, she felt a bulging in her vagina. The cervix had opened suddenly. She delivered a three-quarter-pound fetus just minutes after getting to the hospital.

Both Patricias had cervical incompetence. They shared a common diagnosis and a common goal in their third pregnancy—to have a healthy child. For Patricia W., it would be her second healthy child; for Pat O., her first. To each of them, I outlined the choices of treatment:

- *Choice 1*. Weekly vaginal examinations would take place throughout pregnancy. If cervical weakening were noticed, the mother would be treated with bed rest with legs elevated.
- *Choice 2*. A surgical procedure would be performed on the cervix. In this procedure, called *cerclage*, the cervix is constricted with a suture made of nonabsorbable materials.

Choice 2 leads to two more choices:

- *Choice 2A*. The cerclage would be done before pregnancy. This is called *preconceptional cerclage*. The mother would spend two days in the hospital. After one month of healing, she could become pregnant. The advantage of a preconceptional cerclage is that the patient doesn't have to worry about the operation's causing the pregnancy to miscarry.
- *Choice 2B*. The cerclage would be performed at about fourteen weeks of pregnancy. This is called *postconceptional cerclage*. The risk of spontaneous miscarriage is over by this time, but the procedure itself might cause a miscarriage.

Each of these choices, 2A and 2B, carries two more choices, which, again, the patient has to make herself.

- *Choice 2C*. The cerclage suture would be removed either at about 38 weeks or when labor starts. The advantage of removal of the suture is that the patient then has a good chance of vaginal delivery. The disadvantage is that if further pregnancies are desired, the cerclage must be done again.
- *Choice 2D*. The cerclage suture would be left in place and the baby delivered by cesarean section. The advantage here is that the mother would be able to have further pregnancies using her successful cerclage, which would not have to be replaced. The disadvantage, of course, is the risk carried by any abdominal surgery, along with a longer recovery period after the birth.

Patricia W. said, "I can't possibly stay in bed again. I felt like I was a prisoner. And now Nila needs me. I can't expect Bill to take her to school and pick her up every day.

"I can't see doing the operation before I get pregnant. What if I can't get pregnant? We'll do the operation at the end of three months. Bill will stay home and take care of Nila while I'm in the hospital.

"Of course, I'll want you to take the stitch out. We only want two children anyway. I'd prefer to deliver vaginally and go home after two days. I hate hospitals."

Pat O. said, "I'd be afraid that the operation would somehow hurt the baby. I'd like it to be over with before I get pregnant. Tom and I want more children. I'd rather have the cesarean section; at least we'll be able to do that a few more times. Anyway, even if you take the stitch out, I might not be able to deliver vaginally."

At 38 weeks, I cut out Patricia W.'s cerclage suture. She went into labor the very same day, and she delivered Aaron vaginally. In the same week, I left in Pat O.'s cerclage and delivered Thomas, Jr., by cesarean section.

The Patricias made different decisions, but each Patricia successfully reached her own particular goal.

G.G.P.

# 31. Herpes Infection

Herpes simplex infection has been described as a new plague, and I would be surprised if the majority of readers had not at least heard of this disease. Many may have read about the possibility of birth defects or death in children born to mothers with herpes. But too little knowledge about the problem can lead to unnecessary worry, so it's important to get the facts straight about herpes and pregnancy.

"Herpes" is the common term for any infection caused by the herpes simplex virus. There are two strains of the virus that can cause disease in humans, and either strain may cause lesions on either the mouth or the genitals. *Herpes simplex virus type 1 (HSV-1)* is generally responsible for cold sores, or fever blisters. In the majority of cases it is *herpes simplex virus type 2 (HSV-2)* that causes painful blistering sores on the cervix, vagina, or external genital area. It is this genital herpes and its implications for pregnancy and childbirth that concern us here.

HSV-2 is usually spread by sexual intercourse and is now probably the most common venereal disease in the country, infecting an estimated 500,000 new victims a year. Because it is caused by a virus, not by bacteria, it cannot be killed by antibiotics. In fact, at present there is no known cure for it.

A person exposed to herpes (we refer explicitly, from here on, to genital herpes) will often have flulike symptoms at first—swollen lymph glands, fever, and achy muscles. Within a week, a tingling or itching may occur in the genital area. Painful blisters that may break and become encrusted then develop. Usually all symptoms, including the sores, disappear within ten to twenty days, no matter what treatment is used. The virus may still be active for somewhat longer, however.

After the initial attack subsides, a person is said to have a "latent" herpes infection. Many of those infected never experience a sore again; but in perhaps as many as 60 percent, the sores may reappear at any time, especially around a woman's menstrual period or at times of stress.

A doctor can diagnose herpes for certain only when the sores are present, by looking for their characteristic appearance and sending a cotton-tipped swab of the secretions from the sores for a viral culture. In women, a swab is also taken of the cervix, as sores there may not be easily noticed. A Pap smear is performed as well as a microscopic examination of the cells, which may reveal changes characteristic of herpes.

If a woman has an active herpes infection at the time of delivery, her baby may be exposed to the herpes while passing through the vagina. Sometimes the baby is not infected; sometimes a localized skin infection develops, and the baby recovers completely. However, the infection may become generalized, or disseminated, in the baby and cause severe abnormalities or even death.

It must be emphasized, however, that these problems can be prevented by appropriate medical care. If an active infection is present at the time of labor or has only recently cleared up, the infant may be delivered by cesarean; this can almost always prevent exposure to the virus. Even if a woman has had episodes of herpes in the past, the chances of the baby's developing a herpes infection are very small as long as the virus is not active around the time of delivery. Fortunately, active infections are relatively rare during the latter part of pregnancy.

The following cases illustrate the usual method of handling genital herpes infections during the last trimester of pregnancy.

Sylvia B. was in her seventh month of pregnancy when she developed very painful sores on her labia. When I examined her, the sores appeared to be very tiny ulcers, less than one-eighth of an inch in diameter, and were very sensitive and painful to the touch. I suspected that they were caused by the herpes virus and told Sylvia that she probably had herpes, but that a viral culture and a Pap smear were necessary to confirm the diagnosis. We discussed the fact that herpes cannot be cured but that several things could be done to make her more comfortable, such as sitz baths followed by the application of a topical anesthetic.

The next day, after I received the results of the culture, I called Sylvia and told her she did indeed have herpes. We discussed the need for preventing the baby from coming into contact with the virus, and I outlined my plans for the rest of her pregnancy.

When she went into labor, or if the amniotic sac ruptured, she was to come to the hospital immediately. If it had been more than a month since she had had any sores or evidence of active virus, then the likelihood of the baby's catching the virus during a vaginal delivery would be extremely small. However, if it had been less than a month since a sore was present, a cesarean would be necessary within four to six hours after the membranes ruptured, so that the baby would not contract the virus.

Sylvia's sores were gone in about twelve days, typical for this virus. As the pregnancy progressed, I did weekly viral cultures and Pap smears. After three weeks, there was no more evidence of the virus. Sylvia went into labor at term, more than eight weeks after the original sores had appeared. Her labor and delivery were uncomplicated, and she had a beautiful, healthy baby girl. That was two years ago, and Sylvia has had no recurrence of herpes since.

When Anne C. first came to see me in her eighth week of pregnancy, she knew she had had two episodes of genital herpes in the previous year, but she had no sores when I examined her. Because of her history of herpes, I obtained a culture of her cervix and a Pap smear at this visit, but neither showed any evidence of the virus. I repeated the culture and smear at 36 weeks' gestation, but again there was no sign of herpes, and Anne gave birth to a healthy baby boy three weeks later.

Genital herpes infections are indeed becoming more common, and it is important to understand what the disease is, how it is transmitted, and how it can be treated. It is especially urgent that herpes infections be promptly diagnosed in women who are pregnant or who are considering having children, and it is imperative that any pregnant woman who knows she has had herpes inform her doctor. Given careful observation and proper medical supervision, women with genital herpes *can* have healthy babies.

P.A.H.

# Part Six

❧

# Getting Ready for the Blessed Event

BELIEVE IT OR NOT, YOUR FIRST MONTH OF PREGNANCY ISN'T too early to start thinking about the day you'll become the parent of the child you've just begun to carry. There are certain important decisions to be made, and key questions that must be asked—early on: Will you have "natural" childbirth? *Where* will you deliver your baby? Who will provide guidance during your pregnancy and attend you during the delivery? Will the baby's father play a major role?

Only the parents can answer these questions for themselves. To help you arrive at *your* answers, the following four chapters examine these important issues.

# 32. Prepared Childbirth Today

Today, women take "prepared childbirth" for granted. With the help of its techniques and philosophy, they can be active, alert participants in their babies' births. This was far from the case when today's new mothers were born.

Thirty years ago, when a woman went to the hospital to have her baby, she expected to be treated not as a participant in the birth of her child but as a patient—almost as an object, passively accepting the care of the doctor and nurses attending her. She could also expect to be heavily sedated, often for a considerable period of time. What's more, she was unlikely to question these expectations; this was what it was like to give birth.

Prepared childbirth as women know it today did not become an option overnight. The medical establishment was slow to accept it and, indeed, the zealotry of some of the movement's advocates has somewhat inhibited its evolution.

Gradually, awareness of the dangers of depressant drugs to the baby and increasing sensitivity to the mother's needs have led to the development of many methods of "prepared childbirth." One of the first was the method originated by Dr. Grantly Dick-Read of England. He taught special breathing techniques to be used by his pregnant patients in order to reduce the feelings of pain in labor; practice in advance helped make those techniques truly effective.

Gradually, the inaccurate early term "natural childbirth" was replaced with the more realistic term "prepared childbirth." It was observed that prepared-childbirth women not only had less pain and required fewer drugs in labor, but their labors were faster and their deliveries easier.

Practice in advance received particular emphasis at the Pavlov Institute in Russia in the late 1940s and early 1950s. Using Pavlovian principles of conditioned responses, prepared-childbirth classes conditioned the pregnant women. Intensive training meant that correct breathing responses in the laboring mother could more easily be called into play by the labor "coach." The technique was similar to calling a football play by numbers and having all the players know what to do.

Dr. Fernand Lamaze refined these principles further in France during the 1950s; gradually, our modern concept of prepared-childbirth classes evolved and began to spread.

I have just finished reading a book called *Natural Childbirth the Swiss Way*, by Esther Marilus (Prentice-Hall). Ms. Marilus describes modifications of the Lamaze method, which include more detailed gymnastic preparation and varied breathing techniques. The author believes that the variable controlled breathing that is taught in Switzerland is an improvement over the classical Lamaze breathing. I don't know whether or not it is better, but it is appropriate that we try to improve our classical preparations.

We have entered a new time when the basics have been accomplished and we are free to explore, refine, and perfect the methods that were so revolutionary such a short time ago.

G.G.P.

# 33. Home Versus Hospital

My first experience with home delivery occurred during my very first year in private practice. I had finished my residency in obstetrics and gynecology, I was appointed to the faculty of the medical college, and I felt well-trained and eager.

One evening in early winter, I received a desperate call from Charlie C., whom I had never met. "Doctor Panter, you must come quickly—my wife is having our baby and we can't get a doctor to come!"

I asked, "Why isn't she in the hospital?" and Charlie answered, "The contractions started coming so quickly, and Stephanie knows the baby is coming soon. This is our third child."

"Call an ambulance," I advised seriously. "They can take her to the nearest hospital." And Charlie answered, "They won't come to our house. You *must* come. We heard that you live near us."

"But I'm in my office," I said. "It will be thirty minutes before I can get there."

"There's no one else," Charlie urged.

I left my office immediately and drove as quickly as I could. It was dark out, but somehow I found the secluded cottage in the woods.

A young man was sitting on the dark porch, playing mournful modern jazz on the clarinet. He motioned me into the house with his clarinet, without missing a note.

"Is Mrs. C. okay?" I asked worriedly, somewhat out of breath because of my rush. He pointed his clarinet up the stairs inside.

I ran upstairs to the single bedroom on the second floor of the modest cottage. Under a single overhead bare bulb, Stephanie C. was knitting, propped up on two pillows in the center of a double bed. It didn't need a trained obstetrician to see that she had already delivered. The baby was snuggled against her, nursing, in the crook of her arm.

On the night table I spied a small book on delivering a baby at home. "Why, you *planned* to deliver this baby at home," I said incredulously as the realization overcame me. "Why did you bother to call me? You called me after the baby was born."

"We wanted you to register the birth and get us a birth certificate."

I checked Stephanie and the baby, and they were well. And I said good-bye to Charlie as I passed him, still playing his clarinet, sitting in the darkness at the edge of the front porch.

The home-birth trend has recently become recognizable throughout the United States. During the fifties and sixties, the vast majority of women delivered their babies in the hospital. By 1973, the number of hospital births peaked, home births accounting for only 0.7 percent of all births in the United States. Since then, the number of home births has been rising, and now that figure is probably 2 percent or more.

Intuitively it seems that the out-of-hospital delivery, even in a low-risk population, is not as safe as delivery in the hospital. You can imagine the situation where the umbilical cord is around the baby's neck. As labor progresses, the cord tightens, and the oxygen supply from the placenta to the baby drops. The baby's heart rate drops and provides a signal that immediate correction is necessary to prevent brain damage, or even death.

You might also imagine what could happen at home if there is an *abruptio placentae*. Abruptio placentae is a condition that occurs with no warning. Suddenly, the placenta begins to detach from the uterus, before the baby is born. As abruptio placentae occurs, the blood supply to the fetus may be lessened, causing the baby's heart rate to drop; there may also be external hemorrhaging. It is a very frightening situation, even in the best-equipped hospital. Blood transfusions must be given to the mother while the baby is being delivered.

Besides these possibilities, which actually occur over and over again, statistics gathered by the American College of Obstetricians and Gynecologists reveal substantially higher mortality rates for home births, suggesting that home birth generally is simply not as safe as hospital birth.

The motivations that prompt expecting parents to consider or choose home birth are very understandable. Many couples choose home birth because they wish to preserve the family unit; they wish to have increased parent-child interaction. Others cite unnecessary cesarean sections, the risks of fetal monitoring, and the possibility of infection as reasons for not wanting a hospital delivery.

You, as parents, can—and should—strive to achieve your expectations of childbirth. You can interview your prospective obstetrician to find out about fetal monitoring: Will it be used only during active labor, the time of greatest risk to the fetus, or will it be used all the time? Find out about cesarean sections: When does your obstetrician do a cesarean section? What is the cesarean-section rate in his or her practice? Will you be involved in the decision? What are the hospital's policies about getting the baby to you immediately following the birth? How long can you and your husband be with the baby— alone?

In the past twenty years, the hospital environment has been made increasingly safe for both mother and baby. Maternal mortality in hospitals is almost zero, and perinatal mortality has been reduced by technological advances, such as fetal monitoring, to identify the fetus in trouble.

Many hospitals now have an alternative birth center (ABC) in addition to a traditional labor and delivery suite. Family and friends can attend the birth in the ABC, and the mother can move about in the room during labor. Criteria for admission to the ABC are stringent, however. The mother must be classified as low risk, have had good prenatal care, and attend childbirth classes.

The first priority of childbirth is that it must result in the healthiest possible mother and baby. As modern medicine continues to meet the challenge of this priority, it is to be hoped that it will also meet the challenge of the birthing experience. The problem can be solved in the modern hospital, which will provide a true homelike environment in which the birth process can take place while staying in intimate relationship to the protections of modern science.

G.G.P.

# 34. Choosing a Birth Attendant

Before you decide to have a baby, it's wise to give some thought to selecting a professional to attend the birth. Women today have the opportunity to choose among general or family practitioners, obstetricians, and midwives. Still, approximately 80 percent of the babies born in the United States are delivered by obstetricians, and it can be helpful to understand what their medical training process entails.

Physicians who specialize in obstetrics and gynecology are trained to provide health care specifically to women. Gynecology is the study of women's medical problems not related to pregnancy, while obstetrics is the care of pregnant women. The training of a doctor who is certified to practice obstetrics and gynecology typically includes four years of college; four years of medical school leading to an M.D. degree; one year of internship or first-year postgraduate medical education; three years of specialty training in obstetrics and gynecology, followed by a written examination given by the American Board of Obstetrics and Gynecology; two years practicing as an obstetrician-gynecologist, during which time one is considered to be "board eligible"; and, finally, the successful completion of the board's oral examination, which qualifies a doctor as a board-certified obstetrician-gynecologist. Subspecialty training may follow.

Certification does not guarantee a good physician, but it does provide some assurance that a physician has been deemed competent by a national certifying board. While the current certification includes both obstetrics and gynecology, a physician may choose to limit his or her practice to either one or the other.

While obstetricians provide medical care for most pregnant women in this country, other physicians and practitioners may also care for pregnant women. In some locations, *certified nurse-midwives (CNMs)* may provide obstetrical care under the supervision of an individual obstetrician or group of obstetricians.

The distinction should be made between lay midwives and CNMs. The latter have a background in nursing and receive extensive training in obstetrics, with experience in deciding when a pregnancy or labor is proceeding normally and when further consultation from a physician should be sought. "Lay" midwives, on the other hand, are unlicensed practitioners who have learned "on the job"; the extent of their experience varies. Lay midwives attend only home births, as hospital affiliation can be granted only to those midwives who are certified competent. Some states do not allow lay midwives to practice, although the laws vary from state to state, as do the practices in individual communities. Depending on the location, certified nurse-midwives may provide prenatal care, attend births in a variety of settings (home, hospital, or birth center), provide postpartum care, or dispense contraceptives.

In many locations general practitioners or family practitioners provide obstetrical care. Information about an individual's training and qualifications should be a factor in the choice of any birth attendant.

It is important to identify and select a personal physician prior to the time when an emergency arises, and many factors should be considered in this decision. Many women begin by making a list of the physicians who have been recommended by family or friends. Before deciding to see the same physician as your next-door neighbor, though, consider whether such factors as the physician's age or sex will make a difference to you. If you are new to an area, county or state medical societies may provide the names of physicians who are accepting new patients—or before you move, ask your current doctor for a recommendation or referral.

There are a number of different types of arrangements doctors may choose: solo practice, group practice with other obstetrician-gynecologists, large multispecialty practices (as with prepaid health plans and health department clinics), or staff positions in large university-affiliated medical centers. From a patient's perspective, the obstetrical care provided in each of these different types of practices varies in some important ways.

There are some obstetricians in solo practice who plan to be present for every patient's delivery. Some doctors in solo practice, and most in group practices, however, have some sort of "on-call" arrangement with another doctor or doctors to provide for weekend and night deliveries. In a group practice, one prenatal visit may be arranged with each of the other members of the group in order to allow you to meet the doctor who may be present at the delivery. Although most women would prefer to have "their own" obstetrician present for the delivery, it is not humanly possible for a doctor with a busy practice to work 24 hours a day, seven days a week. However, the call arrangements should be clearly stated by the obstetrician and understood by the patient.

In choosing a physician or midwife, it is also necessary to evaluate his or her office practice and personality. Some questions to consider are: How many weeks must one wait for an appointment? How pleasant is the office setting? Are there educational brochures or books in the waiting room? How long do you have to wait in the office for a scheduled appointment? How capable are the nurses? Will they answer questions? Is billing handled confidentially and efficiently? Are office personnel willing to discuss financial concerns? Is it clear where or whom to call in case of an emergency? Since such questions are often answered only after an office visit, a personal visit is necessary to evaluate both the office setting and the physician's personality and style.

The discussion that occurs during this initial visit is important; it can help you determine if you can have a comfortable working relationship with your doctor. It is important to be able to communicate easily with your physician. Note how the doctor responds to your questions and how you react to the doctor. Do you feel comfortable asking questions? Do you feel rushed? Is the physician really listening to you and addressing both your expressed and your implied concerns?

In my own practice, I do encourage get-acquainted visits, and I try to answer my patients' questions. Sometimes, however, I see new patients who want to interview me at length. Some questions pertaining to the specifics of medical management might be more appropriately discussed as the occasion arises. I think more general questions, such as asking a physician to describe a typical labor and delivery or asking his or her thoughts about prepared childbirth, will give some idea of that doctor's philosophy of care.

One question many women ask concerns the physician's rate of cesarean deliveries. While this information is important, it is necessary to keep in mind that sometimes a cesarean rate is related to the number of high-risk patients a physician treats, or it may be linked to the fact that the hospital where he or she practices is a referral center.

In choosing a physician, remember that two major factors are important in a good doctor-patient relationship: you should feel comfortable relating to the physician, and you should have enough information about skills and training to be able to trust his or her medical judgments and decisions.

P.A.H.

# 35. The Part Daddy Plays

More and more often today, mothers are accompanied during labor and delivery by the fathers of their babies. Although this is a relatively new phenomenon in modern Western culture, it is nearly universal in other cultures for a mother in labor to be accompanied by a supportive friend or family member. That more fathers are taking part in childbirth suggests that such participation fulfills some important needs for parents.

In addition to the psychological benefits of companionship during labor and delivery, a number of medical benefits have also been demonstrated. A recent study done in Guatemala and reported in *The New England Journal of Medicine* found that mothers accompanied during labor by a supportive companion—a *doula*—had lower rates of birth complications and shorter labors than did those who were not. They were also more alert after delivery and they stroked, smiled at, and talked to their infants more within the first hour after birth.

Such studies provide examples of how feelings can influence the way the body functions. When human beings are in a frightening situation, their nervous systems gear up for emergency action—for "fight or flight." The fight-or-flight response certainly makes it easier to battle a tiger, but it makes it more difficult to have a baby. Exhaustion after a "battle" also makes it harder to immediately focus on, and become emotionally attached to, a new baby. The presence of a supportive companion, such as a husband, can make childbirth a less frightening experience for the mother and can help her body respond to it more appropriately.

During labor, the husband or other support person probably makes his greatest contribution just by being there for the mother—and by being understanding and reassuring. He cannot keep labor from being stressful, but he can keep it from being lonely. He can also be an advocate for the mother in an unfamiliar hospital environment and can help her to have a greater sense of control during her labor.

In the early part of *the first stage of labor*, when uterine contractions are irregular and not terribly uncomfortable, the husband primarily provides companionship for his partner. The couple may discuss whether or not it is really labor and how soon to go to the hospital. They will often talk about the expected baby, and the conversation will provide some diversion from the mild contractions. Early labor may also be a time when both partners' anxieties come to the fore; it is helpful to have made hospital preadmission plans, to have a suitcase packed and the obstetrician's phone number written in an easily accessible place, and to have discussed what to do when labor begins.

During the active stage of labor, when uterine contractions are becoming more intense, the husband can help his wife maintain her concentration. He can help her relax her voluntary muscles by letting her know when he notices tension mounting.

During the period of *transition labor*, when the cervix is approaching complete dilation and the contractions seem to be constant and labor never-ending, he can remind her to take the contractions one at a time. This is the time when a laboring woman is most likely to need extra encouragement and reassurance. It is also the time when she may need or request pain relief. It is helpful for the couple to have previously discussed their feelings about the type of medication or anesthesia preferred.

It is also important to remember that the actual experience of labor may be different from what was expected and for both partners to be flexible in terms of what is necessary and recommended by the obstetrician at the time. During this stage, the laboring woman may be more vocal than anticipated, and she may say things that are uncomplimentary or act in an uncharacteristic manner. It is important for the husband to consider these comments in the context of the stress and hard work of the occasion. The husband can provide human contact and support to help his wife from feeling overwhelmed by her intense experience.

*The second stage of labor*—from complete dilation of the cervix to delivery of the baby—involves the husband in a new phase of coaching. This is the time when he can help his wife most by reminding her of their practiced pushes in prenatal classes and by cheering her on. He can help her to keep in mind that the experience is not going to last forever and help her to focus on the goal she is laboring toward—a brand-new baby.

At the time of delivery, the husband stops being a coach and starts being a father. After delivery, the husband can share with his wife the first minutes of getting to know the new human being they have produced. These moments after delivery are a period of intense emotion, a time when parents can begin to form emotional bonds with the infant and strengthen the emotional ties between themselves.

A laboring woman is not the only one who has feelings during childbirth; the father is also in an unfamiliar and stressful situation. He may feel anxious, tired, angry, or frightened. Sometimes he can respond to this anxiety by coaching too rigidly and getting angry with his wife when she fails to perform as expected. Anger more often, but not much more productively, is directed at doctors and nurses. It is important for the husband to make sure he is acting as an advocate for his wife, not as an adversary to others who are trying to care for her. He should also make sure he does not become so anxious himself that his wife ends up having to reassure *him*!

Here are a few tips for success:


• Decide beforehand what the father's role in labor and delivery is going to be. Some men are uncomfortable with the idea of accompanying their wives during labor and delivery, and some women would prefer that their husbands not be there. It is important that each couple decide what is right for them.
• Know your hospital's policies regarding fathers' attendance and consider these policies when choosing a hospital.
• Know what to expect. Understanding labor and delivery can greatly decrease anxiety for mother and father. For this purpose, as well as for others, prepared childbirth classes can be very helpful.

- Talk about feelings related to the birth process with each other beforehand.
- Be flexible. Not everything will go exactly as planned, but under any circumstances, a supportive, understanding husband can make childbirth a better experience. It may be that during a contraction, for example, the mother may feel that any sort of touch is distracting. It is better that the husband try comforting her in other ways than that he feel hurt. It may be that, in spite of all the preparation, a cesarean birth is required, and the husband may be excluded from the operating room. (Again, it is best to have ascertained the hospital's policies prior to labor.) If the husband cannot be present at the cesarean birth, it is better that he try to be warm and supportive in the recovery room and nursery than that he spend too much energy fretting over the experience he has missed.

Even though things seldom go exactly according to plan, the vast majority of couples find that they really do pretty well together during labor and delivery. And many find that the experience draws them closer together in a profound and wonderful way.

P.A.H. (J. Randolph Hillard, M.D., collaborated with his wife on this chapter.)

# Part Seven

૨**

# Birth Day

LIFE DOES NOT ALWAYS PROCEED AS ANTICIPATED, AND that is true in childbirth as in other circumstances. But as Dr. Hillard pointed out in the last chapter, knowing what to expect—understanding the normal process of labor and delivery—can serve not only to prepare you mentally and physically for the events of this momentous day but to decrease anxiety for both parents, as well. And should the *un*expected occur, you will also be much better equipped to cope.

The next seven chapters chart the course of modern, uncomplicated childbirth, starting with the very first sensations signaling the onset of labor. You'll find everything here, from the physiological basics (How does your body know when to begin?) to the hotly debated (Does your baby son really need a circumcision?)—all you need to know about the eventful day, the finale of the nine months' drama.

# 36. When Labor Begins

That last month of pregnancy often seems endless to a mother, who is naturally eager to see the baby she has been carrying for so long. You know, of course, that you must patiently await the onset of labor until nature decides that it will begin. But there are several theories about what starts labor, and it is helpful to know them.

One factor is apparently the *pituitary*, a major endocrine gland located at the base of the brain. *Oxytocin* is a hormone secreted by the posterior lobe of the pituitary gland. When oxytocin is given to pregnant women at the end of pregnancy, it causes uterine contractions. Consequently, if labor must be induced for some special reason, oxytocin is used. (Oxytocin is also sometimes given after normal birth to stimulate the uterus to contract and thus to reduce blood loss during the postpartum period.)

One theory of the origin of labor is that the mother's pituitary starts to release increasing amounts of oxytocin at the end of pregnancy, causing the contractions of labor to start. But no one has been able to prove this, and even if it were so, there is no clue as to what triggers the pituitary to start this important function. However, in a woman who is in labor, the levels of oxytocin in her blood are high, and they do rise appreciably as labor progresses.

Another theory is that the placenta, which forms many hormones in very high concentrations, is responsible for the onset of labor. One of these important hormones is *progesterone*, which relaxes the uterus and prevents it from contracting prematurely. In animals, administering progesterone prolongs pregnancy and, if one takes away the progesterone, labor starts. But in humans, administering progesterone does not prolong pregnancy, nor does the overall level of progesterone drop at the onset of labor. It may be, however, that with the aging of the placenta, a point is reached when the placenta does not produce enough progesterone to prevent uterine contractions from beginning.

The fetus itself may also play a role. *Cortisol* is a hormone produced by the cortex, or outer layer, of the adrenal glands. Animal studies have shown that if the fetus's cortisol production is reduced, the pregnancy will be prolonged. And if excess cortisol is administered to a sheep fetus, it causes premature labor and delivery. Indeed, in human pregnancies with fetuses with congenital defects that inhibit their cortisol production, mothers tend to deliver well beyond their expected time.

And the uterus may be involved, too. During pregnancy, the lining of the uterus develops a special coating called the *decidua*. The placenta is implanted against the decidua, and in the rest of the uterus, the amniotic sac presses against the decidua.

The decidua produces hormonelike substances called *prostaglandins*, which cause uterine contractions, much as oxytocin does. (Prostaglandins may also be used to induce labor.) In natural labor, one can measure increasing levels of prostaglandins in the amniotic fluid and also in the blood of the laboring mother. It is possible that prostaglandins form in the decidua until a critical level is reached, at which time they are released, causing labor to begin. Ordinary aspirin inhibits the production of prostaglandins. We find, in women who must take large doses of aspirin for certain illnesses such as arthritis, that pregnancy tends to be prolonged.

Sexual excitement and orgasm may cause the release of prostaglandins from the decidua, triggering uterine contractions. That is why we caution women who are at risk of premature labor to abstain from sexual stimulation in the last few months of pregnancy.

In any case, it is probably a combination of all these factors—pituitary, placenta, fetus, and uterus—that leads to the onset of normal labor. And there may be other factors that have not been defined as yet. There have been many scientific, and nonscientific, observations.

Experienced labor-room staffs know, for example, that they can expect to be very busy at the time of the full moon. They also report an increased incidence of labor when the barometric pressure falls at the onset of a severe storm. If these are indeed relevant factors, they may be related to pressure phenomena. When the uterus is close to term and ready momentarily for the onset of labor, the cervix becomes thin (effaced) and soft. If the atmospheric pressure falls, the membranes tend to bulge down against the cervix and cause it to stretch.

Drs. J. J. Tsuei, Yiu-Fun Lai, and S. D. Sharma recently described successful induction of labor in 29 of 34 patients by acupuncture of the hands and feet. This finding was reported in one of the leading obstetrical journals, *Obstetrics and Gynecology*. While I do not suggest that you undergo acupuncture to help your labor start, these results certainly suggest that there may be other factors in the initiation of labor, factors we do not yet understand.

G.G.P.

# 37. Pain in Labor and Its Natural Relief

All women pregnant for the first time wonder how painful labor is likely to be. In most cases, labor *is* painful. There are very few exceptions.

A few years ago, Gloria S. came to my office for one of her weekly visits, about ten days before her estimated due date. This was her third pregnancy. We chatted casually as I performed the routine pelvic examination to see if the cervix was effacing or dilating at all in preparation for a coming labor. I was astounded to find that Gloria's cervix was fully dilated: The baby was ready to be born, yet she had not sensed any contractions or felt any pain! I composed myself as I said to her, "You had better call your husband and have him meet us at the hospital. You're ready to have your baby."

I immediately drove Gloria to the hospital. We went quickly through the admissions office. She was taken to the admitting room, where she changed into a hospital gown, and then to the labor and delivery floor. We waited for her husband. As soon as he arrived and changed into a scrub suit, we all went to the delivery room.

During delivery, Gloria kept saying, "But I'm not having any contractions." And I said, "I know, Gloria, but push anyway."

With the second push, a beautiful, healthy baby boy was born. There had not been a single contraction; there had not been any pain. Gloria remarked, "I feel like I've been robbed of my labor." Nevertheless, she had a broad smile on her face.

We all have the fantasy of such a painless labor in our mind's eye. But for the most part, labor is painful, for at least part of the time. In order to understand the methods of pain relief in obstetrics, we must understand the basic physiology of pain. Only then can you know what part you can play to reduce the pain of labor.

The sensation of pain begins when specialized nerve endings are subjected to stimulating energy. These nerve endings are called, as you might expect, *pain receptors*. Pain receptors are present throughout the body and are stimulated by mechanical forces, such as pressure. They also respond to other stimulating energy, such as electrical shock, and to extremes of heat or cold, as well as many chemical stimuli. The property common to all stimuli adequate to excite pain receptors is the threat of damage to the tissue. Once the receptors are stimulated, or excited, they cause mini-electrical pulses to travel back along the nerve fibers to the spinal cord and then up the spinal cord to the brain, where the pain is actually sensed.

The sensation of pain is unpleasant, but it is often protective. For example, the pain of touching a burning-hot stove would cause you to jerk your hand back quickly. In comparison, the other modalities of sense give you more gentle information about your environment.

Different individuals first sense pain at different degrees of excitation of pain receptors. This is called your *pain threshold*. For a given person, the pain threshold is remarkably constant. This means that one person might feel pain with a small pinch, whereas a second person might need a firmer pinch before she feels any pain. The second person is said to have a higher pain threshold. There is no way you can change your own individual pain threshold.

Dr. J. D. Hardy began to study pain in the 1930s in the

physiology department of Cornell University Medical College. Over fifteen years, he published many scientific papers. Dr. Hardy developed an apparatus that would let out a burst of heat over a measured area of skin of the person being studied. Using a 1,000-watt lamp, he was able to focus a spot of heat on the forehead of the subject. He used a shutter like that of a camera to time the exposure of the subject to the heat.

Dr. Hardy found by repeated tests, with increasing intensities of radiant heat, that a threshold for pain can be obtained for any given individual. From there on, it was found that the pain increased in steps called *just noticeable differences*, or *JNDs*. These JND steps were the same for all people. Two JND steps were defined as one pain unit, or *dol*. Dr. Hardy found that there were only 21 JNDs between average threshold and maximum pain. This means that there is a *pain maximum* beyond which you can't feel any more pain, and that maximum (ten and a half dols) is the same for everyone.

Different people start to feel pain at different dols, however, and that's the pain threshold. The average threshold is about two or two and a half dols, but some individuals do not sense pain until five or six dols. It is possible that Gloria S. might have been one of these people with an unusually high threshold.

Dr. Hardy used medical students as his subjects. Using his apparatus, Dr. Hardy was able to train these medical students to describe any painful sensation accurately in terms of dols. Dr. Hardy could flash a brief intensity of known exposure at the forehead of the subject, and the subject would accurately call out, "Seven dols," or whatever degree of pain the stimulus evoked. You can see that these trained subjects were valuable indeed. They could, for instance, be sent to the dentist to have a tooth drilled and tell exactly how many dols of pain they felt.

The most valuable student subjects for this story were the women medical students who became pregnant after they were trained in assessing pain. When these young women were in labor, they could classify labor contractions in terms of dols felt with each contraction. They found that as labor progressed, the number of dols felt with each contraction increased. By the time advanced labor (what is presently called *transition labor*) was occurring, the women noted that the dols were up to nine to ten and a half—and that is at or near the maximum pain that a person can feel. This was, of course, many years ago, before Lamaze or other methods of prepared childbirth were taught to pregnant women.

Another team of researchers, headed by Dr. W. P. Chapman, a physiologist, wanted to know if there was any difference in pain threshold between average and highly emotional individuals. Dr. Chapman used the Hardy apparatus on different people, who were evaluated psychologically. He found that there was no clear difference in the threshold for pain related to emotions. But those who were deemed neurotic reacted more readily to pain; they flinched and grimaced and tightened their muscles more readily and in response to lesser degrees of pain.

How does this all apply to your pain in labor, and what can you do to help reduce the pain of childbirth?

During labor, the contracting uterus forces the baby down against the cervix. This mechanically stimulates pain receptors in the lower uterus. In addition, the contracting uterus presses against the lower abdominal wall and stimulates receptors on the inner surface of that wall. These are the primary pains of labor.

Pain receptors are also sensitive to chemicals—not only chemicals used experimentally but also chemicals that occur naturally in the body. These natural body chemicals can be built up to abnormal levels as a result of prolonged muscle contraction. Prolonged muscle contraction causes muscles to ache and become sore. This pain and aching will occur sooner if the muscles in question lack sufficient oxygen. With good circulation and sufficient oxygen the pain-producing body chemicals will be metabolized away.

There is pain in prolonged muscle contractions, as in the long-distance runner who develops pain in her legs. And there is secondary muscle pain that occurs in muscles that are tensed in reaction to an event. An example of this is the back pain many people get in response to emotional tension, or the stiff-neck pain due to muscle tension that some people develop in reaction to stress.

Now, how can you reduce your own pain in labor? The following guidelines should be helpful.

- Learn the mechanics of labor and delivery so that you can understand the relationship between contractions and progress.
- Know what will happen in labor and delivery, so that you can reduce the stress and anxiety that can cause secondary muscle tension.
- Learn breathing and positioning techniques in labor so that the contraction forces can act and yet reduce the stimulation of the lower-uterine pain receptors.
- Learn breathing techniques in order to allow the uterus to contract with minimal pressure against your lower abdominal wall.
- Learn breathing techniques that will cause optimal oxygenation of tissues and improvement of circulation to metabolize away pain-causing chemicals.
- Learn muscle-relaxing techniques to prevent secondary muscle pain.
- Have your husband also learn to recognize secondary muscle tension, so that he can warn you of it when you are unaware.
- Learn distracting maneuvers to interrupt or diffuse the pain-signaling electrical pulses.

These important points are among the reasons why every pregnant woman should take a preparation-for-labor course. You may not have a totally painless labor, as Gloria S. did, but with these techniques, you should be able to reduce the dols of labor to a very low and far less painful number.

G.G.P.

# 38. Pain: What Your Doctor Can Do

As Dr. Panter has explained in the last chapter, labor is different for every woman. While there are some who say that they never felt a contraction and that labor was not at all painful, most will agree that they did experience pain. Beyond that, the descriptions of the extent and duration of the pain will vary. It is nonetheless something a woman must deal with in one way or another—through prepared-childbirth classes, with the support of a partner, or, if necessary, with medication or anesthesia.

A basic premise behind prepared-childbirth classes is that by reducing fear and tension, pain will also be reduced. Breathing exercises taught in these classes help to distract a laboring woman from the pain by providing another focus for her attention. Relaxation techniques, which help to prevent a woman from tightening other muscles of her body, are also taught. Focusing and relaxation techniques, basically, allow the uterine contractions to do the work that they need to do without opposition.

A partner or labor coach also plays an important role in learning to recognize muscle tension, emphasizing focus on breathing or other distraction techniques, and providing encouragement and general support.

Most women find the breathing and relaxation techniques helpful during labor, and for many women these are sufficient for dealing with the pain. The primary advantage of these methods of coping with pain is that the baby is not exposed to pain-relief medications.

But although prepared-childbirth techniques are helpful for dealing with labor, some women need additional help. It is impossible to predict how an individual woman will experience labor. If she has a particularly long labor, has any complications or problems, or has a low pain threshold, there are other methods of pain relief available. It is good to become familiar with these options before labor starts.

There are a number of factors to consider in determining what other options for pain relief are available. Much depends on the pregnancy and labor itself and whether there are complications or medical problems. The wishes of the laboring woman are also a consideration. The birth environment—the facilities available and the qualifications of the birth attendants—must be taken into account as well.

Medication, usually a narcotic or tranquilizer, given intravenously (into a vein) or intramuscularly (into a muscle), is used frequently. Although medications given to the mother do reach the baby, the type of drug is chosen carefully, and it is administered in small doses, at only certain times during the labor process—usually not during the early or very late stages of labor.

Some physicians utilize a *paracervical block*—an injection of a local anesthetic drug next to the cervix—to provide pain relief during the first stage of labor. Because this has been known to produce a transient slowing of the baby's heart rate, though, it is being used less frequently.

Another form of pain relief is the *continuous epidural block*. A small catheter is inserted into the epidural space around the spinal cord, and a local anesthetic drug is injected, blocking pain sensations from the navel down. An epidural block is a very effective pain reliever and has very little effect on the baby. Complications of epidural anesthesia are also relatively uncommon. A similar technique, a *caudal block*, which involves an injection in the area of the sacrum, or lower back, is another possibility.

Use of nerve blocks requires special training, and they are not available at all hospitals. There are also certain factors—such as infection, blood-clotting problems, or nerve or back conditions—that preclude this type of treatment. An epidural block cannot be given too early in labor, or it may slow the labor process. Because it requires some time to place the catheter properly, this technique is also not useful when delivery is imminent. And an epidural block may alter the sensations of pushing during the second stage of labor, making the necessity of a forceps delivery somewhat more likely. It is possible, incidentally, to use an epidural block for a cesarean delivery; the mother can be awake and alert to greet her newborn, but the pain of the surgery is blocked by the anesthetic.

Other types of regional anesthetic blocks include a *spinal*, or *saddle, block*, which provides numbness in the vaginal area and is useful for forceps deliveries, and a *pudendal block*, which stops pain impulses from the lower vagina and perineum, allowing an episiotomy to be performed. (A local anesthetic may also be injected into the area of the episiotomy only.)

*General anesthesia* is rarely administered for vaginal deliveries today, but it is still used for cesarean births.

Epidural, caudal, and spinal blocks require the injection of a local anesthetic drug around the spinal cord. Although the idea of a needle in the back can be quite frightening, in actuality it is more uncomfortable than painful. If you do have strong feelings about various methods of pain relief in labor, it is best to discuss them ahead of time with your doctor, who will try to answer your questions and will abide by your wishes to the extent that it is medically possible.

Ultimately, it is best to wait and see how labor progresses for you. Be prepared with as much information as you can gather through classes, additional reading, and discussions with your doctor about the options that are available to you.

P.A.H.

# 39. Fetal Monitoring

"I've waited a long time for this pregnancy. I want it to be perfectly natural. I think that Irwin would be frightened if he saw me attached by wires to a lot of electronic gadgetry. Will I really need a monitor when I'm in labor?"

Ellen R. was speaking very frankly about her fears of electronic fetal monitoring. I had known Ellen for a long time; she had been one of my first patients when I started my practice. Now, she was thirty-five years old and pregnant for the first time.

In the past ten years, *electronic fetal monitoring,* or EFM, has become a standard method of monitoring the mother in labor in modern obstetrical hospitals in the United States and in many other countries throughout the world.

The laboring woman starts monitoring her contractions at the onset of labor, using a watch, and can describe the intensity, duration, and frequency to her doctor or midwife. She might say, "The contractions are coming every six minutes, they last 40 seconds, and they only hurt a little bit." The birthing attendant or the patient's husband can also time the contractions and feel their intensity by placing a hand on the mother's abdomen. This monitoring allows the course of labor to be followed, but further monitoring must be done to check the condition of the baby.

It is known that the fetal heart rate (FHR) reflects the amount of oxygen reaching the baby and tells whether or not the baby is distressed. The average normal FHR, both before and during labor, ranges from 120 to 160 beats per minute, about twice the normal rate of an adult's heart. If the blood flow to the baby decreases, or the oxygen reaching the baby lessens, the baby's heart rate slows. When the FHR slows to below 100, it is called *fetal bradycardia.* The lower the FHR, the more ominous a sign of fetal oxygen lack and distress there is.

Fetal bradycardia is categorized as either *transient deceleration* (a momentary slowing of the FHR) or, if it lasts over a minute, *persistent deceleration*—an ominous sign indeed.

Fetal bradycardia is also classified by how it occurs in relation to a uterine contraction. If the deceleration occurs with a contraction, it is called a *variable deceleration.* This is not considered serious and may represent merely the effects of compression of the fetal head with the contraction. More serious is the deceleration that occurs after a contraction, a *late deceleration.*

In the past, the FHR was monitored by the birthing attendant with a stethoscope. About every ten or fifteen minutes during labor, the doctor or nurse would listen to the FHR to note whether it was normal or slow. If fetal bradycardia was detected, it would start a flurry of activity, which often ended in the mother's undergoing a cesarean section, for it was well known that persistent severe reduction in fetal oxygenation would cause brain damage.

It has been shown, however, that late transient deceleration can occur with only mild degrees of reduced oxygen and without brain damage occurring. Therefore, finding late deceleration is an early warning signal that the fetus is in danger—allowing time to institute proper measures to protect the fetus. Since these late transient decelerations can show up suddenly, with any contraction, and since a stethoscope is often not sensitive enough to pick up the FHR during a contraction and does not allow the birthing attendant to interpret the signals fast enough, electronic fetal monitoring (EFM) can provide the best early warning of impending fetal danger.

EFM is therefore a wonderful tool; it is certainly one of the most important of this century's advances in obstetrics. And as it turned out, EFM enabled us to protect Ellen R.'s baby from serious damage while still permitting her to have a vaginal delivery.

Ellen's labor started uneventfully within a few days of her due date. By that time, I had explained the reason for EFM to her, and both she and Irwin had seen the electronic units on their hospital tour. When Ellen arrived in the labor room, the contractions were strong, and they were occurring every three minutes.

An elastic mesh was placed around Ellen's abdomen. Two sensing devices were placed within the mesh, and they were attached by a long, flexible electrical cord to the continuously recording monitor. (The cords are long enough that the mother can move about the labor room while her contractions and the FHR are recorded simultaneously.)

Irwin and Ellen were not nervous as she was attached to the EFM setup. I was there as the monitor began to record. It quickly became obvious that Ellen's baby was showing transient late decelerations. After each contraction, the FHR would slow from 140 beats per minute to 90, for about ten seconds.

I explained the meaning of the tracing to Ellen and Irwin as we placed a light oxygen mask over Ellen's mouth. We needed to increase the amount of oxygen getting to the baby.

I examined Ellen. Her cervix was four centimeters dilated, and the baby's head was descending into the birth canal.

The oxygen helped. The decelerations stopped for the next ten contractions. Then, in spite of oxygen administration, the decelerations returned. This time, they were more severe, with the FHR dropping to 80 and staying there for twenty seconds after each contraction.

We elevated the foot of the labor bed in order to reduce the pressure on the baby's head. But the decelerations continued to occur, and their duration continued to lengthen. Pelvic examination showed that the cervix was six centimeters dilated. We were still hours from delivery.

I displaced the baby's head; that is, I pushed it back up the birth canal. I found that if I pushed the baby up with each contraction, the deceleration would not last as long. This was a sign that the umbilical cord was around the baby's neck. With each contraction, the cord was tightening, and the blood flow through the umbilical cord was being reduced; this reduced the amount of oxygen getting to the baby.

The only way to avoid the need for a cesarean section *and* to keep the baby oxygenated while labor continued was to compensate for the effect of each contraction upon the tension in the umbilical cord. I had to push the head back up the birth canal after each contraction. And we all waited together for the cervix to dilate to ten centimeters. The next two hours passed very slowly, and we were all delighted when a healthy boy weighing eight pounds, four ounces was born. (I was especially pleased, since the baby's parents decided to call him Gideon.)

Only with the moment-to-moment monitoring of the fetal condition, as reflected by the fetal heart rate in relation to the uterine contractions, could this sort of labor management be undertaken. Electronic fetal monitoring provided the early warning signal of fetal distress. It then provided the security that our corrective measures were adequate and that the baby was safe from serious oxygen deprivation. EFM allowed the continuation of labor, which led to a vaginal delivery.

Ellen and Irwin now tell all their pregnant friends, "Get to the hospital early and have the monitor attached as soon

as possible." They show their beautiful, healthy son as an
example of what EFM can help to achieve.

G.G.P.

# 40. The Third Stage of Labor

We all tend to take for granted the third stage of labor. One
evening some months ago, I delivered Sybil and Larry H.'s
daughter at 11:00. While they were joyously discussing the
fact that Samantha's birthday would be March 29, it would
turn out that I would not leave the delivery room until March
30. For even though the first stage of labor and the delivery
were perfectly normal, the third stage of labor was not progressing as it should.

Sybil was 37 years old, and Samantha was her first child.
The pregnancy had been normal. Labor started at about noon
on March 29. The contractions were strong and regular from
the start. By 3:30 P.M., on admission to the hospital, the cervix
was dilated three centimeters. The baby was lined up perfectly
in the birth canal. Sybil was doing her Lamaze breathing very
well. With no difficulties, but with much hard work on her
part, the cervix was fully dilated at 10:05 P.M. The first stage
of labor had lasted ten hours.

By definition and convention, labor is divided into three
distinct stages:

*The first stage of labor* begins when the cervix effaces and
dilates in response to uterine contractions. It ends when the
cervix is sufficiently dilated to allow the baby to pass through.
For the average delivery, that dilation is ten centimeters, the
diameter of the average baby's head. (While we generally
interchange the terms *fully dilated* and *ten centimeters*, in
the case of a birth where the baby's head is only nine centimeters in diameter, fully dilated would be nine centimeters.)

The average duration of the first stage of labor in women
having their first child is about twelve hours. In women having

a second or subsequent child, the average duration of the first stage of labor is about seven hours.

*The second stage of labor* begins with full dilation of the cervix and ends with the birth of the baby. This is the stage when the mother pushes down with her contractions as the baby descends down the birth canal.

The average duration of the second stage of labor for first-time mothers is 50 minutes. In later births, the second stage is about twenty minutes, but it can be as little as one push, only seconds in length.

Sybil began to bear down at 10:05 P.M., as soon as she was fully dilated. At first, her pushes were weak and poorly co-ordinated. But as each contraction occurred, she became more and more effective, finally matching beautifully her voluntary pushes with the involuntary contractions provided by nature. By 10:40 P.M., we could see a shock of Samantha's hair as the vagina bulged with the forces of pushing and contractions. Sybil was taken to the delivery room, and Samantha was born at 11:00 P.M. The second stage of labor had lasted 55 minutes.

*The third stage of labor* begins with the delivery of the baby and ends with "delivery"—separation and expulsion—of the placenta.

After the baby has been delivered, the obstetrician or mid-wife feels the uterus through the lower abdomen to be sure that it is firm and contracted. These afterbirth contractions will cause the placenta to separate. Usually, a gush of blood will exit from the vagina as the placenta separates. This gush is the blood that pooled at the site of placental attachment to the uterus while separation was taking place. As the separated placenta begins to move down into the lower part of the uterus and cervix, much like the just-completed passage of the baby during delivery, the uterus rises up in the abdomen.

At this point, your birth attendant asks you to bear down. With one or two gentle pushes, just as you pushed to effect delivery of your baby, you will similarly "deliver" the pla-centa. Your obstetrician might help your pushing by pressing on the uterus with a hand on your lower abdomen. The whole process takes but a few minutes.

During a recent study in Sweden, Dr. Bengt Sorbe found that among 1,513 women, the normal range of third-stage duration was between two minutes, twelve seconds and seventeen and a half minutes.

Larry was holding his daughter. He and Sybil were discussing whom they should call first to announce Samantha's arrival. But the placenta had not yet separated. I glanced at the delivery room clock; fifteen minutes had passed since birth. There had been no gush of blood to signal the placental separation, and I knew that we would soon have a prolonged third stage of labor.

One might wonder why the obstetrician would choose to wait before intervening to remove the placenta. Traditionally, obstetricians have cited fear of introducing infection and thus increasing the chance of fever and complications in the mother in the few days after delivery.

But Dr. Howard Blanchette of the University of Southern California compared 100 women who had manual exploration of the uterus after childbirth with 100 controls. Dr. Blanchette found that there was no statistically significant difference in the incidence of fever or infection between the women who were explored and the control women.

Why, then, if manual exploration does not increase fever and infection, do we not always just reach up into the uterus and remove the placenta in each woman after she has delivered her baby? There are two reasons. One is the basic rule that there is no reason to interfere with natural processes. Second, manual removal of the placenta requires anesthesia. Such intervention can be a very uncomfortable intrusion into what should be a quiet, reflective time for new parents.

Still, as the third stage of labor lengthens, there is a risk of hemorrhage from the placental edge. When the third stage reaches 30 minutes, the risk factor rises considerably. A third stage of labor's lasting more than 30 minutes is sufficiently out of the ordinary to necessitate active intervention to remove the placenta.

I made sure that Sybil's regional anesthetic block was working. I asked the nurse to administer a tranquilizer, and I double-checked the time that had elapsed since delivery. Then

I sat down and waited. When the nurse told me that 30 minutes had passed, I gently reached into the anesthetized vagina and up into the uterus. The placenta separated easily and slid into the lower uterine segment. With one gentle push, Sybil expelled it.

I removed my gown and gloves and, as I left the delivery room, I realized that because of the prolonged third stage of labor, it was already the day after Samantha's birthday.

G.G.P.

# 41. The Episiotomy Debate

One of the most common questions my patients ask during their prenatal visits is, "Will I need an episiotomy?" The answer depends on many factors.

Although I do not consider episiotomy to be a necessary routine procedure, many physicians do, and it is a subject of continuing controversy. There are situations when I believe the procedure is indeed called for, but this is a medical judgment that must be made at the actual time of delivery. It cannot be determined with absolute certainty beforehand. This is why many obstetricians become upset with women who demand during prenatal visits that no episiotomy be performed.

In order to understand why a physician may choose to perform an episiotomy, it is necessary to know exactly what the procedure entails and the reasons for it.

An *episiotomy* is an incision made in the skin between the opening of the vagina and the anus immediately prior to vaginal delivery. The purpose of the incision is to enlarge the vaginal opening. Before the procedure is performed, some type of anesthesia is usually administered to numb the lower vagina and the perineum, the skin around the vaginal opening. After the area is numb and the baby's head has begun to distend beyond the outlet of the vagina and three to four centimeters of the infant's head is showing (crowning), a small incision, usually two to three centimeters long, is made.

The incision is one of two types: *median* (midline) or *mediolateral*. A median episiotomy begins in the center of the vaginal opening and is directed straight toward the anus. This type of incision may be somewhat more likely to tear into the rectum than is a mediolateral episiotomy, which begins centrally but is then directed toward one side. If a larger opening is necessary to allow for delivery of a large baby or an infant in the breech position, a physician may choose to perform a mediolateral rather than a median incision. If the cut should extend into the rectum, however, it is repaired immediately and usually heals quickly and without complication.

Bleeding from an episiotomy is usually minimal, because the incision is made just prior to delivery, and it is generally a small one. After the baby is delivered and the umbilical cord cut, the physician will inspect the episiotomy to check for extensions or tears. After the placenta is delivered, the episiotomy is repaired. The area is usually still numb from the anesthetic, but if it is not, more anesthesia may be used. The sutures (stitches) are usually of the type that dissolve or are absorbed and do not need to be removed, so there is no need to worry about painful stitch removal.

Most obstetricians feel that an episiotomy is necessary for forceps deliveries, babies that are delivered in a breech (buttocks first) position, large babies, and in some cases, deliveries after prolonged labor. There is less agreement on whether an episiotomy is routinely necessary. It has been estimated that between 50 and 90 percent of primigravidas (women delivering their first baby), and from 25 to 30 percent of multigravidas (women having their second or subsequent delivery) undergo episiotomy in the United States today. Obstetricians who feel that an episiotomy is a necessary procedure cite various benefits:

- If no incision is made, the skin may tear. A straight surgical incision is preferable to a jagged tear, which may not heal as quickly or as well. An episiotomy is also less likely to extend into the rectum than is a tear or laceration, which may result if no incision is made.

• The baby's head is spared the pressure of stretching and distending the vaginal opening.

• An episiotomy and proper repair may better preserve pelvic tissues than if the vagina and pelvic muscles were torn or greatly stretched.

Although these points may well be valid, scientific data are currently not available to prove them. It is also not necessarily an automatic conclusion that tears will result if no episiotomy is performed.

Massaging and stretching the vaginal tissues prior to labor and delivery may help to minimize the likelihood of lacerations, although this, too, lacks scientific proof. Prepared-childbirth classes may be helpful in teaching breathing techniques that may allow a laboring women to push slowly and carefully to deliver the baby in a controlled manner, rather than pushing frantically at a time when tears may result. Obstetricians and birth attendants who do not routinely perform episiotomies know and utilize techniques such as keeping the baby's head flexed (chin tucked on chest), gradually stretching and massaging the vaginal opening, or using warm compresses; all these techniques are designed to minimize the possibility of an episiotomy or tearing of tissues.

As with any surgical procedure, some problems may arise when an episiotomy is performed, and the benefits must be weighed against the potential risks. The problems may include:

• the possible extension of the incision into the rectum;
• possible difficulty in repairing the episiotomy;
• increased blood loss from the incision itself;
• pain at the site of the incision;
• the potential for swelling or perhaps infection;
• the possibility that painful intercourse may result from improper healing of the episiotomy.

When an episiotomy is necessary, the resulting pain may be quite mild or it may require treatment with various pain medications, medicated pads, ointments, sprays, ice, or heat lamps. Sitz baths may also help to alleviate the discomfort.

Most women who have had an episiotomy would agree that the absence of stitches would be a big advantage and would certainly improve comfort in the postpartum period. On the other hand, obstetricians and birth attendants would agree that if a moderate or large tear seems to be inevitable in spite of precautions, an episiotomy is preferable.

As with any questions or concerns about pregnancy and birth, it is certainly advisable for a patient to ask her doctor at a prenatal visit about his or her philosophy regarding episiotomies. Some physicians will reassure their patients that they believe the procedure is a wise and safe precaution that prevents certain problems. Others will answer that although they do not perform episiotomies as a matter of course, they do think it may be necessary on some occasions. I ask my patients to have confidence in my medical judgment at the time of delivery, since that is when the decision must be made. I do take into consideration most women's preference to avoid any unnecessary discomfort during delivery and the postpartum period and weigh this against the advantages of performing an episiotomy at the time.

I also find that many women have exaggerated fears of episiotomy when they are pregnant. They are frightened of the pain associated with incisions and are worried that the procedure might somehow adversely affect their delivery. Looking back, however, most women I have asked admitted that their episiotomy was not such a "big deal" after all, and was, in fact, a very minor part of their total birth experience.

P.A.H.

# 42. Decision: Circumcision?

Circumcision is not as much a routine procedure as it was a generation or two ago. More and more parents are weighing the pros and cons before deciding whether or not to have their male infants circumcised. Before making a decision, however, it is necessary to know exactly what the procedure involves and what the advantages and disadvantages might be.

Circumcision is a procedure to surgically remove the foreskin, the loose skin at the end of the penis covering the glans. It is one of the most commonly performed surgical operations in this country, and one that many parents consider to be routinely necessary or mistakenly believe is required by hospital policy or even law.

The majority of male infants in the United States are circumcised. Jews and Moslems have a religious basis for choosing circumcision, but for most others, the reasons for having a son circumcised include a combination of social concerns and a belief in the medical benefits of the operation. Some people think, for example, that circumcision prevents infection, disease, and even cancer. The American Academy of Pediatrics has stated, however, that "routine circumcision of the newborn infant lacks medical justification." The benefits of circumcision have not conclusively been found to outweigh the potential risks.

Circumcision may make it easier to keep the penis clean. The practice of circumcision was less common in this country prior to World War I. It became much more common and even routine after American physicians serving in World Wars I and II began to see that some uncircumcised men developed problems resulting from the war-zone conditions that made good personal hygiene extremely difficult. Cleaning the uncircumcised penis is not difficult, however, and can be taught to young boys quite easily.

Although circumcision has been reported to be possibly protective against the development of cancer of the penis, good hygiene probably offers equal protection. The risk of developing cancer of the penis is small, and that risk is probably less than the risk of a major complication associated with circumcision. Recent research also indicates that cancer of the cervix in women is not associated with an uncircumcised partner.

It has also been argued that circumcision prevents the development of *phimosis*, a condition in which the foreskin is tight and cannot be retracted. Phimosis may indeed necessitate circumcision in an older boy or man. It should be noted, though, that almost all newborn boys have foreskins that cannot be retracted. The need for circumcision in adulthood is certainly prevented by the routine circumcision of newborns, but the necessity of later circumcision is rare, and circumcision as a preventive measure subjects hundreds of thousands of babies to an operation they would most likely never need.

Although circumcision is usually a safe and simple operation, there are potential risks. The most frequent complication is hemorrhage or greater-than-expected blood loss. In some instances, only direct pressure is required to stop the bleeding, although it may require a special pressure dressing, stitches or, less commonly, a blood transfusion.

Infection of the wound may also result; such infection is usually mild but may require antibiotics. The sensitive glans of the penis is exposed to the irritation from wet diapers and may become raw or develop sores. Although most infections or irritations of the glans heal without problems, scarring of the *urethral meatus*, the opening from which urine exits, may occur.

The surgery itself may result in problems, such as the removal of too much skin from the shaft of the penis, incomplete removal of the foreskin, or nicking, cutting, or burning the penis or scrotum. Although such problems happen infrequently, exactly *how* infrequently is unknown. Very rarely, circumcision had led to complications that resulted in death.

Many different methods of circumcision are used, and the amount of foreskin removed varies. Often, a plastic or metal device designed specifically for circumcision is used.

The operation is most often performed without anesthesia.

The infant is restrained on a papooselike board, and although the procedure is relatively simple and quick, almost all infants cry with discomfort or pain. It is obvious that the argument that "babies don't feel the circumcision" is belied by infants' responses: babies cry, and they may have a bowel movement, become flushed, or vomit. Some physicians now use a *nerve block*, or local anesthesia, to numb the penis, similar to the way a dentist numbs the gums before filling a cavity. Although this technique is not widely employed, physicians who do use it routinely are impressed with the way in which the babies tolerate circumcision without crying.

Jewish infants are generally circumcised in the eighth day of life by a *mohel*, who is trained to perform the ritual circumcision. For other infants, an obstetrician, urologist, or pediatrician may do the surgery. It is usually performed after the first 24 hours of life and before the baby goes home from the hospital, although a small or premature infant may not be circumcised until any medical complications of prematurity have been resolved.

Often, the obstetrician is the operating surgeon, although it has been argued that the baby's pediatrician or primary-care physician might be a more appropriate person to do the procedure, since obstetricians rarely see the results of their surgery in follow-up visits. Questions about the care of infants, including how to care for the circumcised or uncircumcised penis, are most often answered by the pediatrician or family physician, who can also provide information about how to teach good penile hygiene.

Parents should carefully assess their own feelings and thoughts about circumcision, preferably prior to delivery, so that they are not called on to make this decision hurriedly after the baby's birth. Questions to examine include:

- Has the father of the baby been circumcised himself, and what are the prevailing social norms? Some parents feel that they want their son to look like Dad. Others are concerned that they do not want their son to look different from his classmates in the showers at gym classes. Many

parents, though, are willing to explain differences between father and son and between their son and his friends.
- What does the pediatrician advise? What about the obstetrician? Many physicians believe quite strongly in circumcision, while others feel that the medical evidence is not conclusive and that the decision should be based on personal and social considerations.
- Who would perform the operation? The answer to this question varies and depends on religious considerations and the usual medical practices of a community.
- Is an anesthetic used?
- How important is this issue to each individual parent or to the couple?

Although there appears to be little medical justification for routine circimcision, certainly hundreds of thousands of men have no recollection of this early "trauma," and any psychological consequences would be impossible to define. It is up to each parent to examine the data at hand, assess his or her own feelings, and make an informed decision.

P.A.H.

# Part Eight

ೊ

# When Complications Arise

WHILE NO TWO CHILDBIRTHS ARE EXACTLY ALIKE OR PRO-
ceed at exactly the same pace, most are relatively routine; the
birth attendant's role is chiefly that of watchful waiting (and
monitoring), of keeping a trained eye on mother and child and
standing ready to assist if needed. But in some instances, there
are distinct departures, untoward events that demand definite
medical action in order to ward off a critical threat to mother or
baby. This is, indeed, the major reason for having an obstetrician who has followed your pregnancy with you or on instant
call (which is the situation at in-hospital birthing centers with
registered nurse-midwives in basic attendance).

Such circumstances may include unusual positions of the
baby within the uterus, significant differences from the norm
in the timing of events surrounding the onset of labor, and
other conditions that may interfere with normal vaginal delivery. The next eight chapters examine these special circum-

stances and explain how current medical techniques can come to the rescue.

# 43. Placenta Previa

Pregnant women and obstetricians generally agree that the best way to give birth is as naturally as possible. For the most part it is best to minimize the use of drugs and special procedures and allow the natural birth process to take its course. The main purpose of the modern hospital is to stand by and be available for the rare special situations where active intervention may be necessary. At those particular times, judicious use of drugs and up-to-date equipment and personnel enables babies to be born whole and healthy with minimal trauma to their mothers.

I was reminded of this during a recent Memorial Day weekend. I received an urgent telephone call from Linda M. on Sunday morning. I had delivered her previous two daughters, and each occasion was a wonderful experience for us all. Both former pregnancies were uncomplicated, and the labors were relatively short. Linda had to work in labor, of course, but she was well prepared and required minimal coaching. She seemed to know what to do instinctively, and she and her husband, Randy, and I shared the exhilaration of her births joyously.

This was Linda's third pregnancy, and she and Randy were hoping for a boy. But this time it was different. It was six weeks before her due date, and something was happening. I could hear considerable fright in her voice when she said, "I just woke up and there was a gush of fluid in the bed! And I think that I'm contracting. I'm not even due for almost two more months!"

Linda had good reason to be concerned: She was in premature labor, with ruptured membranes. With ruptured membranes, we could not stop labor, and she would deliver later that day. I told her to get to the hospital as quickly as possible, and I started to dress as soon as I hung up the phone.

By the time we met in the labor room, Linda was contracting every four minutes. The fetus was active, and the fetal heart rate was normal, at 140 beats per minute. I examined her abdomen and saw that the baby was presenting head first; I estimated its weight to be about four pounds. I told Linda and Randy of these findings as I prepared to do a pelvic examination; I reassured them that while the baby was obviously small and early, babies in that weight range do very well with modern nursery care.

There was more bloody show than usual as I performed the pelvic examination. Linda was five centimeters dilated, about half the dilation necessary before delivery can take place. But much to my surprise, I could feel the edge of the placenta alongside the baby's head. And the bleeding increased with the examination.

Normally, the placenta implants in the upper part of the uterus, so that it does not interfere with the birth process. When it implants very low, it can interfere with birth, and it is called *placenta previa*. Placenta previa is a condition that usually makes itself known with painless vaginal bleeding during the seventh or eighth month of pregnancy. Most patients who have this condition are treated with a few days of bed rest in a hospital. The bleeding usually stops, and the pregnancy can continue until term. If more bleeding occurs and the baby is large enough, a cesarean is performed.

If the placenta previa covers the entire cervical opening, it is called a *complete* placenta previa. A complete placenta previa blocks the passage of the baby, and the baby must be delivered by cesarean section. If the placenta covers just part of the opening of the cervix it is called a *partial* placenta previa. Sometimes, as labor progresses, the placental edge moves aside and the baby can pass through the cervix. But the placental edge can start to bleed, and the mother can lose too much blood. When this happens, again an emergency cesarean section is necessary.

Linda had a partial placenta previa, and it was just beginning to bleed. It was time for active intervention, and the labor-room staff of nurses and doctors began to work very fast. We explained what we were doing as we went along.

If we could stop the bleeding, we could allow labor to progress toward a vaginal delivery. But if the bleeding continued, a cesarean section would be necessary. We alerted the operating team to stand by. We would try to stop the bleeding by compressing the bleeding placental edge.

Oxytocin infusion was started in the intravenous line. Oxytocin is a drug that strengthens contractions and forces the baby down the birth canal with greater force. I was hoping that the head of the baby would thus compress the placental edge and stop the bleeding.

A monitor was placed on Linda's abdomen. It measured the contractions so that we could watch the effect of the oxytocin. But more important, it also monitored the baby's heart rate. If we were strengthening the contractions, we wanted to be very certain that we were not causing trauma to the baby. Stress to the baby would have shown up as a drop in the fetal heart rate, which was continuously displayed by the monitor.

The contractions became stronger, and the bleeding slowed considerably. The active intervention was working. But Linda, without great discomfort until now, began to complain of severe pains. These contractions were much stronger than she was used to. An anesthesiologist gave her an epidural anesthetic. (*Epidural anesthesia* is a form of regional anesthesia in which pain is blocked below a certain level in the body. The level is controlled by the amount of a Novocain-like drug injected just outside the spinal cord.)

Now everything was under control. Linda was comfortable in spite of the stronger, oxytocin-stimulated contractions, which were forcing the baby's head against the placental edge and stopping the bleeding. And the fetal monitor showed that the contractions were not stressing the baby. There was nothing to do but wait.

The next hour seemed very long. The cervix dilated and the placental edge moved aside. We reached ten centimeters and moved to the delivery room. Linda was told to push. The baby began to descend through the birth canal.

She was scrawny, and their third girl, but no one was disappointed when her vigorous cry filled the room.

G.G.P.

# 44. Premature Rupture of the Membranes

One Friday evening, at about 10:00 P.M., I was contacted by my answering service and asked to call Anne S. Anne was 32 years old and pregnant with her second child. Almost exactly three years ago, she had delivered her first baby, Oliver. That pregnancy and delivery were uncomplicated, and I was looking forward to another straightforward delivery. In fact, I was anticipating an easier time, since first labors and deliveries are generally harder and longer than successive labors and deliveries. Anne was now about twelve days before her due date, and I thought she was calling to tell me that labor had started.

I telephoned the number given to me by my answering service, and Anne answered. "I'm afraid I've sprung a leak," she said. "We were just finishing dinner at my mother's house, and I felt a warm fluid coming out of my vagina." I asked her if she was having any contractions, and she said no. I explained to Anne that she had *premature rupture of membranes*, or *PROM* in medical abbreviation. I told her to get a good sleep and to call me if she awoke in labor.

Premature rupture of membranes means that the amniotic membrane, which surrounds the baby and the amniotic fluid, develops a small hole or tear, and amniotic fluid leaks out before the onset of labor. PROM has nothing to do with having a premature baby. The *premature* part of PROM simply refers to the fact that the membranes have broken open, or ruptured, before contractions have started. PROM occurs in 15 percent of pregnant women, and no one knows exactly why it happens.

The amniotic membranes that make up the gestational sac are transparent. One can actually look through an intact sac and see the baby inside, floating in its amniotic fluid. Sometimes the membranes are ruptured by a violent kick by the baby. Usually they rupture during active labor, when the pressure within the uterus builds up to a very high level and forces the sac to bulge down the birth canal. And sometimes the membranes will rupture as the result of severe trauma to the uterus, as one might have in a serious car accident. But for the most part, in PROM, no specific cause can be found for the event.

I had told Anne to go home to sleep so that she would be well rested to meet the labor that I expected. Eighty-five percent of women with PROM at term (near the due date) will spontaneously begin labor within 24 hours of the release of amniotic fluid. I, too, went right to sleep, in preparation for the middle-of-the-night phone call that I expected.

I awoke Saturday morning well rested and surprised that there had been no phone call to wake me. I called Anne's home, and Spencer, her husband, answered with a sleepy voice, "No, no labor; she's still sleeping. Why don't you talk to her yourself?" I did and told Anne that she and Spencer should go to the hospital. Because she had not gone into spontaneous labor, I would have to induce labor. As hours pass after premature rupture of membranes, with no labor or delivery, certain risks begin to threaten both the mother and the baby.

Besides enclosing the fetus, the amniotic membranes serve as a barrier to prevent bacteria or other infectious agents from entering the amniotic fluid and reaching the baby. The normal vagina has an ecological balance of many different bacteria and fungi. This population of microscopic organisms serves a useful and important purpose: It keeps the vaginal interior healthy and resistant to infection from the outside. But the vaginal organisms, necessary to the health of the vagina, are dangerous to the lining of the uterus and to the fetus.

When the membranes rupture, the vaginal organisms can move upward to cause an infection within the amniotic sac. Such an infection is dangerous, because the bacteria can move from the sac into the mother's bloodstream, as well as the baby's.

Years ago, such events meant almost certain death to both mother and baby. Fortunately, with the use of antibiotics, it is very rare for a mother to die as a result of amniotic infection.

But even with antibiotics, such infection can still threaten the life of the baby. We are fortunate, however, that the migration of the vaginal bacteria up into the nonprotected amniotic sac is a relatively slow process. The risk of neonatal infection is about 1 percent for about the first 24 hours after rupture of membranes. It then rises abruptly to 3 percent and continues to rise to about 5 percent by 48 hours.

I met Spencer and Anne in the labor room at the hospital and explained all this to them in detail. While it was fair to wait about twelve hours for spontaneous labor to begin, we could wait no longer. We wanted the baby to be born before the time of rising risk, twelve more hours away. Anne was now among the 2.5 percent of pregnant women who find themselves in this high-risk situation.

One might ask why these women are not given antibiotics at this time, prophylactically, as a preventive. It has been shown that antibiotics prevent or delay infection in the mother. But the antibiotics do not seem to stop the amniotic sac infection, which precedes the baby's great risk. And without antibiotics, the mother will usually show an elevated temperature and white blood cell count as amniotic infection develops, while antibiotics will suppress these reactions; we use these signs as a signal for immediate intervention to get the baby out of the infected sac. The antibiotics at this time, then, do not protect the baby, and they mask the danger signals.

Anne had normal temperature, and her bloood count was normal. She was not given antibiotics, so that her temperature could be measured every hour to see if the baby was still safe. She was an excellent candidate for induction of labor, because her first labor and delivery had been normal.

Each step in this reasoning was explained to Anne and Spencer. The option of not inducing labor and hoping for spontaneous labor would not be sensible; if infection should occur without labor far along, a cesarean section would have to be done. Induction of labor was the prudent choice at this time, and our goal was to have delivery occur before 24 hours after the premature rupture of membranes.

An intravenous infusion was started. It would serve two

purposes: to keep Anne from becoming dehydrated during labor, and to provide the route by which the labor-inducing drug would be given.

*Oxytocin* is a hormone that is produced in the pituitary gland, a small gland at the base of the brain. For reasons we don't know, oxytocin is released into the bloodstream in greater amounts when someone is in labor. It circulates through the blood and it is picked up at special places in the uterus called *oxytocin receptor sites.* The oxytocin causes the release of hormonelike substances called *prostaglandins*, which act on the uterine muscle to cause contractions. Oxytocin is very potent, and it is administered slowly. The induced labor, properly done, starts slowly, like a natural labor.

We monitored the contractions and the fetal heart rate on a fetal monitor, so that we could see the progression of contractions and so that we could be sure that the fetus was not stressed by them.

Soon, Anne was in labor. As the contractions became more frequent and stronger, I alerted the pediatric staff that a pediatrician would have to be present at birth to examine the baby for signs of infection and to take cultures to see if any bacteria had reached the baby. Three hours later, Anne gave birth to a daughter, Sarah.

"There's no sign of infection," said the pediatrician. "Of course, we'll have to wait for the results of the cultures," he added, as he handed Sarah to Anne, just as I tied the last suture of her episiotomy. And, indeed, by the time she was ready to go home, the cultures were officially reported to be negative.

G.G.P.

# 45. Labor: Too Early . . .

Hilary K. started her labor at 10:00 in the morning and delivered a six-pound baby girl at 4:10 in the afternoon. This labor was uneventful, and it progressed just as expected. But we were all particularly happy when the baby was born—for it was Hilary's third labor during this pregnancy. The other two labors had had to be stopped, because they were inappropriately early.

Hilary and Barry K. are in their early thirties. I had delivered their first baby, Joshua, three years ago. That pregnancy and labor were uneventful, and we had no reason to suspect that there would be any problems when Hilary became pregnant this time.

I was therefore very surprised to get a middle-of-the-night phone call from Hilary, two and a half months before her due date. "Dr. Panter—I just woke up and I'm having labor pains. And I feel a pressure down in my pelvis. It feels just like when Joshua was born!"

Barry's voice was on their extension phone. "She had a contraction at 1:05, then 1:18, 1:33, and 1:47, and then we called you."

"Are they hurting?" I asked. "They certainly are," Hilary answered, suddenly gasping, "Barry—I'm having another one!" I told them to get right to the hospital; I would meet them there.

When spontaneous labor occurs too early, there is increased risk of fetal death and damage. A study by researchers at the John Radcliffe Hospital at the University of Oxford, published in the *British Medical Journal*, showed that premature births were responsible for 85 percent of all infant mortality not related to birth defects.

Many studies have demonstrated that certain drugs will effectively suppress preterm labor and prolong the pregnancy. However, preterm labor must be diagnosed as early as possible, so that the contractions may be stopped before labor becomes irreversible. To diagnose preterm labor, one must observe uterine contractions ten minutes or less apart, along with progressive cervical effacement and dilation.

I met Hilary and Barry at the hospital. Barry's chart of contractions showed that the contractions were occurring every eight to twelve minutes. I could easily confirm his record of contractions just by feeling Hilary's abdomen and noting the tension building up in the uterus as each contraction occurred. The uterus—about two inches in height above Hilary's umbilicus—was 27 weeks, or six and a half months, in size.

A vaginal examination showed that the cervix was 50 percent effaced—it had thinned out to half of its normal length. And with each contraction I could feel the baby's head pressing down against the cervix. Hilary was in premature, or preterm, labor. We transferred her immediately to the labor floor, where she could be monitored closely and where intravenous treatment could be given.

While there are many treatments advocated to stop premature labor, the exact mechanism by which premature labor occurs has not yet been defined.

Dr. Barry Schwarz, associate professor of obstetrics and gynecology at the University of Texas Southwestern Medical School in Dallas, discussed the subject at a conference sponsored by the March of Dimes Birth Defects Foundation. Dr. Schwarz pointed out that before any particular therapy can be singled out as the treatment of choice, the underlying physiology should be understood more clearly.

Premature labor might be due either to a trigger for normal labor occurring too early or to an entirely abnormal mechanism. Dr. Schwarz believes that it is an abnormal mechanism, possibly related to infection, that causes premature labor. Dr. Schwarz quoted a study at Ninewells Hospital in Dundee, Scotland, where pathologists studied the placentas and membranes of women who had premature labor and delivery for no obvious reasons. There was microscopic evidence of infection in 60 percent of these cases, suggesting that infection might be the underlying mechanism.

Dr. Schwarz believes that infection of the membranes will reduce the diffusion of oxygen from the mother's tissues to the membranes. (The membranes have no blood supply of their own, so they rely not on actively delivered oxygen but on diffusing oxygen.) Without sufficient oxygen, the membranes release *prostaglandins*, the hormonelike substances that cause the uterus to contract and start labor. But this theory is not yet proved. And 40 percent of the placentas and membranes in the study he cited showed no evidence of infection.

Dr. Robert Creasy studied preterm births at the University of California at San Francisco School of Medicine. Dr. Creasy attempted to identify those women who are at greatest risk of having preterm labor. Based on the pregnant woman's medical history, Dr. Creasy classifies her risk of having a preterm delivery as low, medium, or high. The woman is screened again at 26 to 28 weeks of pregnancy and is reassigned to a different category if necessary.

Of 966 patients studied by this method, 59 women—or 6 percent—delivered preterm (between 20 and 38 weeks). Of the 125 who were classified as high risk at 26 to 28 weeks, 38 delivered preterm, accounting for 64 percent of all the preterm births. The incidence of preterm deliveries was 2 percent, 5 percent, and 30 percent in the low-, medium-, and high-risk groups, respectively.

Because of her good medical history, Hilary K. would have been classified as low risk. Yet she was definitely in premature labor and required immediate treatment.

We placed an external fetal and contraction monitor on Hilary's abdomen so that we could see the effects of the treatment on the contractions and on the baby. The hospital bed was cranked at an angle so that her feet would be higher than her head. This is called the *Trendelenberg position*. It serves to reduce the pressure of the baby's head against the cervix.

A tocolytic drug was given intravenously. *Tocolytic* means contraction- or pressure-inhibiting. We watched the contraction monitor eagerly. The contractions became less and less frequent and less and less strong, and we knew that the medicine was working. Hilary stayed on the labor floor with the monitor attached to her for 24 hours. During that time, we were able to switch her to an oral form of her tocolytic medicine, and soon she was able to eat and walk around.

She was discharged on oral tablets, three times a day. We were twelve weeks from the due date, and the baby weighed only about two pounds at that time; it needed to grow and develop considerably. There were strict instructions: rest, no housework, no sex, and regular office visits. It worked very well, and we celebrated each passing week as a very special anniversary.

About six weeks later—six weeks before the due date—Hilary confided to me at one of her regular office visits, "The contractions started again two days ago—but I stopped them myself. I didn't want to go back to the hospital, so I got into bed and I took two extra tablets. I would have called you if the contractions had continued."

My upset at her making this decision on her own was assuaged somewhat by my relief at her success in stopping her second premature labor. I would have prescribed the same myself—bed rest, Trendelenberg's position, and adjusting the drug dosage to match the need. A patient should, however, always call her doctor in cases like this; Hilary was fortunate that her treatment coincided with what I would have prescribed, and that it worked.

Three weeks later, we reached the thirty-seventh week. We had planned long ago that at this time, we would start to reduce the tocolytic drug. The baby weighed almost six pounds. Barry and Hilary could safely resume their sex life together. We knew that the third labor would be appropriate.

G.G.P.

# 46. . . . Or Too Late

Judy K. stated emphatically that she was ready to have her baby. In fact, she had been ready for the past ten days, since her due date. She was tired of answering her friends who commented, "What? No baby yet!" And she was tired of sitting at home waiting for labor to begin.

Judy's plight is not uncommon. I have yet to meet a woman who was not tired of being pregnant by the time her due date had passed. Many women feel big and uncomfortable during the last trimester and look forward to being "unpregnant." The due date, or "estimated date of confinement" (EDC), is often interpreted as a guaranteed day of delivery, but this is unfortunately often not the case.

Although the average pregnancy lasts 40 weeks, or 280 days, the duration is calculated from the first day of the last menstrual period, and the normal range is anywhere between 38 and 42 weeks. The EDC is determined by using Nägele's rule, by which one adds seven days to the first day of the last menstrual period and counts back three months. For example, if the last menstrual period began on June 14, the EDC would be March 21 of the next calendar year. I try to emphasize to my patients that the EDC is an approximate date, and that delivery from two weeks prior to the due date to two weeks after is normal. Only about 10 percent of pregnancies last more than 42 weeks from the onset of the last menstrual period, and they are designated *postterm* or *postdates* pregnancies.

Aside from the pregnant woman's concerns about comfort and the difficulty involved in waiting patiently for the delivery, physicians take special note of pregnancies that last beyond 42 weeks. Although the *majority* of babies born at 42-plus weeks have no problems, there is statistically an increased risk that the baby *will* have problems, even in the absence of identifiable maternal factors.

Some of these problems have to do with abnormalities of growth. Most postdates infants will continue to be well nourished, but some, who are large at 40 weeks, will be even larger at 43 weeks, and they may have difficulty in their journey through the mother's pelvis. There may even be such a disproportion between the size of the infant and the mother's bony pelvis that a cesarean birth is necessary.

On the other hand, some infants who are postterm outgrow the ability of the placenta to supply nourishment, and they may actually lose weight. At birth, these "dysmature" infants typically appear to have long, thin limbs, peeling skin, and long fingernails. They are also at increased risk of suffering distress at birth.

Distress is sometimes associated with the passage of fetal stool, called *meconium*, during labor. In one study, approximately 40 percent of postdates infants passed meconium before delivery. When this occurs, it alerts the obstetrician attending the birth to watch carefully for other signs of fetal distress. This is best accomplished by closely monitoring the fetal heart rate during labor with an electronic fetal monitor.

An additional problem can occur at the time of delivery when meconium has been passed into the amniotic fluid: The infant can aspirate the meconium, sucking the thick, sticky material into the lungs with the first few breaths. This can physically obstruct the air passageways as well as lead to pneumonia. To prevent this problem, suction tubing is used right at birth to thoroughly remove any meconium from the back of the baby's throat before the first breath is taken.

Although it is becoming increasingly rare, some postterm pregnancies result in unexplained stillbirths. It is in the attempt to prevent stillbirth that obstetricians recommend very close follow-up and sometimes specialized testing for postterm pregnancies.

An initial problem in monitoring women who have passed their due dates is to identify those who are truly postterm. Some women are very sure of the date of onset of their last menstrual period. Others may have had irregular periods or may have taken oral contraceptives prior to conception, making it more difficult to ascertain the date of conception.

An examination of the size of the uterus in early pregnancy will help to confirm the EDC as calculated from the last menstrual period. Additional factors, such as the detection of fetal heart tones with a stethoscope by twenty weeks' gestation and the appropriateness of uterine size throughout the second trimester, help to confirm the accuracy of the EDC. If a woman has not visited a physician early in her pregnancy, it is more difficult to confirm her due date, although an ultrasound examination prior to 28 weeks may be helpful. If the due date has been established and the pregnancy continues beyond 42 weeks, the problem then is to detect those fetuses that are affected by undernourishment or placental insufficiency.

Obstetricians' opinions about the best way to test for fetal well-being vary. Some check urinary or blood substances, including estriol or human placental lactogen (HPL), as potential indicators. Falling levels of these substances may indicate a problem and the need to deliver the infant quickly. Other tests, such as the fetal activity test or the oxytocin-challenge test (OCT), may be used either alone or in conjunction with measurements of estriol or HPL. In these tests, the baby's heart rate is observed in response to either fetal movements or mild contractions induced by the drug oxytocin.

If there is no evidence of fetal distress (if the OCT is normally reactive or the estriol or HPL levels are within normal limits), most obstetricians will elect to await spontaneous labor. The tests are often repeated once or twice a week, until labor occurs on its own or the test results are abnormal. If there is evidence of fetal distress, labor is usually induced with intravenous oxytocin. Whether labor begins spontaneously or is induced, most obstetricians feel that electronic fetal monitoring is particularly important in postterm pregnancies in order to detect signs of fetal distress during labor.

Many women who are past due wonder if they will need a cesarean delivery. It may be necessary in a postterm pregnancy, but for the same reasons that indicate a cesarean birth in a term pregnancy: disproportion (when the infant is too large to be born vaginally), severe fetal distress, or other emergency conditions such as abnormal bleeding or prolapse of the umbilical cord.

Judy K. and I were relatively sure of her due date, which had passed ten days before. She understood that the date was only approximate, but waiting was becoming increasingly difficult. Since both she and the baby appeared to be doing well, I saw no reason to interfere by inducing labor. Her cervix had begun to dilate, and I predicted labor would begin within a week. Five days later labor had still not begun, and she returned for a fetal-activity test. The test showed no signs of fetal distress, so it was not necessary to induce labor.

Judy's labor began the following day. Because of the potential risks, electronic fetal monitoring was used to check how the baby was tolerating labor. When the membranes ruptured, meconium was detected in the amniotic fluid, and I explained to Judy and her husband that I would suction the baby's throat immediately upon birth, so that the meconium would not enter the lungs. A short time later, a healthy baby boy weighing eight pounds ten ounces was born. Judy and her husband agreed that he was well worth the wait.

P.A.H.

# 47. The Case for Forceps

Katherine and her husband had not anticipated that their second baby would enter the world buttocks first. Just six days earlier, the baby had been in the usual birth position—head first—but sometime before labor began, the fetus had turned. We were monitoring the situation closely and were prepared for a cesarean birth should problems arise. Fortunately, however, labor was progressing well.

Shortly before the delivery, I explained that I planned to use obstetrical forceps to assist in delivering the baby's head. In a breech presentation, the baby's head does not have as much time to mold to the shape of the mother's pelvis, and forceps offer some protection. After the baby's body was delivered, I carefully positioned the forceps around his head. A healthy boy, Joshua, was born moments later.

Some women are afraid that forceps might harm the baby, and they are unclear about the nature of the instrument and how and when it is used. *Obstetrical forceps* are instruments used to assist in the vaginal delivery of an infant. The forceps are made of metal and are similar in shape to a pair of salad tongs. Although the instruments vary considerably in size and shape, their basic design is similar.

Forceps consist of two parts, called *branches*, that fit together or lock where they cross. Each branch is introduced separately into the vagina and manuevered into the appropriate position. The part that is inserted into the vagina is called the blade, although it is not at all sharp. Nor does it consist of claws or hooks. It does have two curves: the cephalic, which conforms to the shape of the fetal head, and the pelvic, which follows the natural curve of the mother's birth canal.

Forceps serve two main functions: traction, pulling the baby down and out through the vagina to the vaginal outlet; and rotation, helping the baby's head to turn during the normal course of labor. Although forceps do compress the baby's head somewhat, a careful obstetrician will make sure that the instrument is correctly positioned and will not use undue force. Forceps are also designed to minimize compression—they are not attached to the baby's head, but support it firmly between the two blades.

A great deal of medical judgment and skill are necessary for a physician to decide when a forceps delivery is called for. Forceps can sometimes be used to allow a vaginal delivery rather than a cesarean. In general, however, the difficult and possibly traumatic forceps deliveries of the past are now accomplished by cesareans. The potential for risk to the fetus as well as to the mother must always be considered in the decision.

Today, there are fewer situations in which obstetricians elect to use forceps than in the past. Physicians agree that certain conditions must be met before they will consider a forceps delivery. The cervix must be fully dilated, and the baby's head must have descended well into the pelvis. If the head is at the vaginal opening and is positioned face down with the scalp visible, what is termed a *low*, or *outlet*, *forceps* delivery may be possible. If the head has not descended to the vaginal outlet or is turned somewhat, then the procedure is considered a *midforceps* delivery. *High forceps* deliveries, in which the head has not become engaged in the pelvis, are no longer performed. The situation of a baby's presenting in a breech position is somewhat different; the forceps are used to assist delivery of the "aftercoming" head.

An obstetrician may recommend an *outlet forceps* delivery in some situations to shorten the second stage of labor (after the cervix has fully dilated). Although an arbitrary time period of, for example, two hours, to allow the second stage of labor to continue is generally no longer considered valid, the progress of labor must include both the continuing descent of the baby's head and a normal fetal heart rate. If this is the case, then there is probably no need to intervene.

There are situations, however, where medical problems arise and it is preferable that the mother not bear down. The use of forceps can then speed the delivery. Forceps may also be used sometimes to expedite the delivery of an infant experiencing distress as reflected in the deceleration of the fetal heart rate. In addition, forceps may be employed to assist a mother who is extremely fatigued and having difficulty expelling the baby, or a woman who has had an epidural anesthetic that has diminished her urge to push. Forceps may also be used to protect the more fragile head of a premature infant at the time of delivery or to assist in the delivery of a baby in breech presentation.

If the baby's head fails to rotate as it moves through the mother's pelvis, a *midforceps delivery* may be required. This situation may occur as a result of the shape of the mother's pelvis, or sometimes with an epidural anesthetic. Occasionally it may indicate some cephalopelvic disproportion—that is, the mother's pelvis may not be large enough to accommodate the infant's head. A skilled obstetrician must then decide whether to attempt a forceps delivery or to perform a cesarean instead. Sometimes a physician will attempt a trial forceps delivery; the forceps are applied, and gentle traction or rotation is begun. If excessive force is required or difficulties encountered, the forceps are removed and the delivery is accomplished by cesarean.

While an outlet forceps delivery poses little risk for the baby, some obstetricians feel that a midforceps delivery exposes the fetus to too much risk. Others believe that midforceps deliveries are warranted in carefully selected cases because they enable some women to avoid cesareans.

Generally, when a forceps delivery is performed, anesthesia is required. Physicians often use an *epidural*, or spinal, nerve block, with anesthetic drugs injected around the spinal canal to block the nerve sensations from the pelvis. This eliminates pain from the area just below the navel. In a *pudendal* nerve block, an anesthetic drug blocks the sensations that travel via the pudendal nerve from the vaginal and perineal areas only. Since the use of forceps requires additional stretch of the vaginal and perineal tissues, an episiotomy is necessary. It is usually performed after the forceps have been applied to assist descent or rotation of the baby's head but before the head is delivered.

The baby who has entered the world with the aid of forceps may have some pressure marks across cheeks and forehead. Some bruising may be evident, but it will resolve with time. Forceps babies often have elongated heads; this is not due to the forceps themselves but is related to the reasons that a forceps delivery was necessary to begin with. Molding of the fetal head to fit the mother's pelvis occurs to some extent in almost all deliveries, but if the baby is a "tight fit," more molding and elongation may occur. In such cases, the baby's head would be elongated even if delivered spontaneously. The baby may be such a snug fit that an obstetrician elects to assist the delivery with forceps, in which case it may be incorrectly assumed that the forceps caused the molding.

A woman whose baby is delivered by forceps should not feel that she has failed. It is better for her to have developed a good relationship with her obstetrician, so that when or if a forceps delivery is recommended and the reasons explained, she can trust and rely on her doctor's judgment and medical skill.

P.A.H.

# 48. Breech Presentation

It was a routine monthly obstetrical checkup for Mary Ellen D. She was 32 weeks pregnant, and she was eagerly awaiting her first child. Mary Ellen was on the examining table, and I was measuring and examining her uterus and the baby by feeling her abdomen. "What's the position of the baby?" she asked.

Mary Ellen was making a common mistake with obstetrical terminology. She wanted to know what part of the baby was pointing down toward the birth canal, the part of the baby that would come first. This is called the *presentation* of the baby, while *position* refers to whether the presentation is to the right or to the left or forward or backward. As I explained this to her, my examining hands identified the hard, round head of the baby in the upper part of the uterus. "You have a breech presentation," I answered.

Mary Ellen's face actually turned pale, and her voice became tremulous. "Doctor, isn't that something terrible?" We started a series of discussions about breech presentations and breech births.

The *breech* is the lower part of the baby. Breech presentation occurs in 3 to 4 percent of deliveries. But breech presentation is a common, transient finding earlier in pregnancy. As the fetus develops and the pregnancy progresses, the fetus has to adapt to the shape of the uterus. At about 30 to 32 weeks of pregnancy, with about ten weeks left until delivery, about 30 percent of fetuses will be found as breech presentations. With the passage of time and growth of the fetus, most babies will turn to become *vertex*, or head-first, presentations. I explained to Mary Ellen that we would wait to see what happened at her future visits.

There are three basic variations of breech presentation. The most common is the *frank breech*. In the frank breech, the legs of the baby are bent straight up at the hips, with the knees straight. Fortunately, babies are very flexible, since in the frank-breech presentation the feet of the baby are all the way up by the baby's cheeks.

Less common is the *complete breech*. In the complete breech, the knees of the baby are flexed; the baby is in a sitting position, with legs folded in front.

The third type of breech presentation is the *incomplete breech*, or *footling breech*. In this type, one or both feet or knees lie below the buttocks of the baby. This can present as either a single footling or a double footling, depending on whether one or both feet are coming first.

The incomplete or footling breech is almost always delivered by cesarean section, since in this sort of breech, the baby can easily get tangled with the umbilical cord. Since the breech baby does not fill the birth canal fully, as would a head coming first, the cord has room to slip down. This serious complication is called a *prolapsed cord*, and it requires immediate delivery before the forces of labor cause the cord to become compressed, interfering with the oxygen supply to the baby.

In addition, the incomplete breech creates an inefficient dilating wedge against the cervix. The feet and body of the baby might slip through the cervix before it has dilated enough to accommodate the head of the baby, which may then become trapped. That would be a terrible complication indeed.

Fortunately, Mary Ellen did not have a footling breech. But at her next visit, at 36 weeks, one month before her due date, she still had a breech presentation. On vaginal examination, it felt like a frank breech. We started her weekly visits.

The main feature to remember in managing a breech birth is that the largest part of the newborn is the baby's head. When a baby is presenting head first, labor may be observed for many hours while the forward-coming head molds and adapts to the pelvic architecture. The obstetrician can be confident that if the head finally comes through, the body of the baby will generally slip through with ease.

In a breech birth, successively larger portions of the fetus are born, with the largest part, the head, coming last. And once the baby has been delivered to its navel, the umbilical cord is compressed by the chest and head in the birth canal. From that moment on, the baby is no longer getting oxygen transfer from the placenta. This means that from the time the belly is born, the baby's head must be born within two to three minutes or serious oxygen deprivation can occur. There is no time for molding of the head; it must fit through the bony pelvis quickly and easily, if a vaginal delivery is to be successful.

Of course, if a mother has had previous births of normal-size children with no complications, her pelvis is considered to have been tested. Such a woman is a good candidate for the vaginal delivery of a breech presentation.

But Mary Ellen's pelvis had not been tested. We would have to know for certain that her pelvis was roomy enough before we could consider a vaginal delivery.

At 38 weeks of pregnancy, the weekly pelvic exam revealed that the cervix was starting to efface and dilate, a sign that labor would soon start. The baby was still in a frank breech presentation.

I explained to Mary Ellen that we would have to obtain a pelvic series, a set of three X-ray views of the bony pelvis. Those would enable me to make actual measurements of the upper pelvis, in order to be sure that the head could fit readily. If the measurements showed that the pelvis was too small, a cesarean would have to be done.

Usually, tall women have roomy pelvic architecture. Mary Ellen was five feet seven inches tall. Her pelvic measurements were above the limits necessary to attempt vaginal delivery in breech position.

At each visit, I reviewed the essential instructions. Mary Ellen knew that with a breech, she must rush to the hospital at the very earliest signs of labor, so she could be examined to see if a prolapsed cord were present. Mary Ellen also knew that she would have to receive regional anesthesia prior to delivery. (Anesthesia is necessary in the event that the head does not line up well for delivery.)

By the time Mary Ellen started labor, she was an expert in breech birth. Mary Ellen had the assurance that her pelvis was large enough. She came to the hospital early. Pelvic exam showed a frank breech, the best kind for a vaginal delivery. There was no prolapsed cord, so that labor could continue safely. Of course, the baby was monitored continually to be sure that cord or oxygen problems were not developing.

At seven centimeters dilation, even though she was in control of her contractions with her Lamaze breathing, Mary Ellen was given an epidural anesthetic. With this she would be able to push when necessary. And if I had to intervene, I would not waste precious moments administering and waiting for anesthesia.

The head was well formed and was delivered easily. Mary Ellen had given birth to a lovely daughter.

G.G.P.

# 49. Why a Cesarean?

Many women are concerned about the rising rate of cesarean births, births in which the baby is surgically removed from the uterus. At the hospital where I practice, approximately one in five babies was born by cesarean last year. It is true that because our hospital is a referral center, we have a higher percentage of patients who have medical problems and are considered high risk than does the average community hospital. The rate of cesarean births might therefore be expected to be somewhat higher than average. Still, the percentage of cesarean deliveries in the United States tripled between the late 1960s and the late 1970s. Both patients and physicians are concerned about the increase and are debating the reasons behind it.

To address this issue, the National Institute of Child Health and Human Development organized the Task Force on Cesarean Childbirth, a group composed of professionals from the fields of obstetrics, psychology, law, family practice, and sociology, as well as concerned health-care consumers. Their consensus statement, published in October 1981, confirmed that there is still much to learn about cesarean birth and that the rising rate is cause for concern. It also explored the reasons women are having more cesarean deliveries.

Studies have suggested that cesarean birth improves the chances for a healthy baby in some medically complicated pregnancies. Conditions that had in the past required a difficult forceps delivery are now often dealt with by cesarean delivery.

The operation itself, although not without risk, has become safer because of improvements in anesthesia, the use of antibiotics to treat infection, the wider availability of blood for transfusion, and better medical treatment of illnesses such as diabetes and high blood pressure. Partly because it is safer now, physicians may be more willing to perform the operation if the condition of the baby might be improved by a cesarean birth. The major reasons for cesarean delivery include dystocia, breech presentation, fetal distress, and repeat cesarean.

*Dystocia*—literally, "difficult labor"—is a term used to describe an abnormally slow progression of labor. This may be caused by several factors: The uterus may not be contracting strongly enough, or the contractions may be uncoordinated, so that labor progresses slowly; the fetus may be too large to fit through the mother's bony pelvis (fetal-pelvic disproportion); or the fetus may be turned in an unusual way, with face or perhaps shoulder engaged within the pelvis.

The task force found that dystocia was a problem prompting nearly a third of the cesarean births surveyed. There is little information to document whether a cesarean birth is actually better for the baby than a vaginal delivery when the problem is dysfunctional labor. Information does suggest that cesarean birth does not necessarily increase the survival rates of normal-size babies. The task force recommended such measures as allowing the laboring woman to rest (sometimes with the aid of mild sedation), allowing her to walk around, or using oxytocin, a medication that stimulates uterine contractions, in an effort to avoid a cesarean delivery. More research is needed to study those and other factors such as the effects of a support person on the progress of labor.

A baby in *breech presentation* is upside down. Less than 4 percent of term infants actually enter the world bottom or feet first, even though a higher percentage are breech in earlier stages of the pregnancy. A number of factors may contribute to a breech presentation, including uterine abnormalities, such as fibroid tumors, and fetal factors, such as an unusually large head. But often, the reason for a breech presentation is unknown prior to labor or even after the baby has been born.

It is interesting to note that in 1970, almost 12 percent of breech babies were delivered by cesarean. By 1978, the figure had risen to 60 percent. Research does suggest that cesarean delivery may be safer than vaginal delivery for premature breech babies. The same is probably true for breech babies who are quite large or who have their feet ahead of their buttocks (footling breech). The best method of delivery for average-size babies in breech presentation is still uncertain;

more research is needed to determine just what is best for them.

*Fetal distress* is a problem that is being diagnosed more frequently (although it is not clear if it is actually occurring more frequently), partly as a result of the increased use of fetal monitoring. Since fetal distress can lead to brain damage, it is important to detect the condition as soon as possible. Further studies are needed to allow obstetricians to make this diagnosis more accurately. If the diagnosis of fetal distress could be made with more certainty, perhaps fewer cesareans would be indicated.

The task force's figures showed that *repeat cesarean deliveries* account for nearly a third of the cesareans performed and for 25 to 30 percent of the increase in the cesarean birthrate. More than 98 percent of the women who had had a cesarean birth delivered by cesarean in subsequent pregnancies.

The initial reason for this recommendation was the concern that the uterus, weakened by the surgical incision, might rupture during labor. This was more valid when the incision left a vertical scar in the uterus, which did make it more susceptible to rupture. More common today is the low transverse (side-to-side) incision, which is significantly stronger. It is also of note that the type of incision made in the uterus may not be the same as that made in the skin; a woman can have a vertical skin scar and a low transverse uterine scar. It is the uterine scar that is important for uterine wall strength, not the skin scar.

The task force concluded that because the risks to some mothers and babies of allowing a trial labor and attempt at vaginal delivery are small, "the practice of routine repeat cesarean birth is open to question."

Guidelines have been suggested for determining the circumstances in which a woman who has had a cesarean birth could potentially attempt a vaginal delivery in a subsequent pregnancy. These include the provisions that she give birth in a hospital with appropriate facilities, staff, and anesthesia capabilities for a prompt emergency cesarean; that the previous uterine incision is known to have been of the low-transverse type; and that the patient and her family have been informed about the risks and benefits of an attempted vaginal delivery rather than a repeat cesarean.

The task force also addressed a number of other issues regarding cesarean delivery. It recommended that:

- the type of anesthesia be discussed by the patient and her obstetrician and anesthesiologist;
- prenatal parent education include information on the possibility of a cesarean birth and the technical procedures involved;
- when the decision to perform a cesarean delivery is made during labor, the obstetrician discuss the reasons for the decision to the extent that time and circumstances permit;
- hospitals be encouraged to liberalize their policies of allowing the father or other support person to attend the cesarean birth;
- a healthy baby not be routinely separated from the parents following a cesarean delivery.

The task force also emphasized that there is a need for much further study regarding the behavioral effects of cesarean birth on the mother and family, as well as on infant development, in an effort to improve the health care of both pregnant women and their babies.

P.A.H.

# 50. Postpartum Infection

A loving couple prepares for childbirth in great detail. Books are read, diet is zealously optimized, vitamins are taken, exercises are done, and breathing techniques are practiced. Every possible precaution is observed. The couple go to the hospital secure that they have done everything correctly in preparation for birth. In most cases, no complications ensue, but occasionally something does go wrong. Fortunately, when a complication occurs, it is usually correctable. Yet even the smallest complication of childbirth is a bona fide reason for concern.

I received a phone call on a recent Saturday night from a husband concerned about his wife, who had just delivered her first baby by cesarean four days before: "Joan is still running the fever she developed after giving birth; I was at home having dinner and she called to tell me that her eight o'clock temperature was 101 degreees. They won't give her the baby until her temperature is normal, and she's discouraged. Isn't there anything else you can do? I wish medicine could be more like a business, where solutions can be quick and straightforward."

Joan's husband, Tom, was frustrated because it seemed that his wife wasn't getting any better. I told him that Joan was indeed improving and that we would meet in her hospital room the following morning to review her condition in detail.

Joan had spent the first 36 hours after birth in the usual way—resting, recuperating, and getting to know her baby. And then her temperature rose to about 101°F. Although she had no specific complaints, when she was examined, her uterus was tender to the touch, far more than normally expected.

Joan had *endometritis*, an infection of the endometrium, the lining of the uterus. In response to the ovulatory cycle each month, the endometrium thickens, developing a specialized lining called the *decidua*, in which a fertilized ovum implants and against which the placenta grows. If fertilization and implantation do not occur, this lining is shed in the monthly menstrual flow. But if a fertilized ovum successfully implants, the decidua is maintained throughout pregnancy and is shed in the *lochia*—the discharge that occurs in the first days and weeks following delivery.

If bacteria gain access to the uterus, the endometrium and decidua may become infected. Fortunately, this is rare prior to delivery—when an infection might spread to the infant—because the narrow cervical canal leading to the uterus is usually filled with a protective mucus plug until shortly before labor begins. But endometritis occurs following 2 to 3 percent of vaginal deliveries, and up to half of women delivering by cesarean may become infected.

Although endometritis is a serious infection, it usually responds to antibiotics within three to four days. In Joan's case, bacterial cultures were taken from her blood, urine, and uterus in order to confirm the diagnosis of the infection, and we started to administer antibiotics intravenously so that they would reach the site of infection in large enough doses and as quickly as possible.

Before modern times, endometritis was the leading cause of death in childbirth; it was the deadly and mysterious "puerperal fever" or "childbed fever," which often reached epidemic proportions in maternity hospitals. Several physicians in the nineteenth century had suggested that the disease was contagious, but the cause could not be determined, and bacteria were as yet unknown.

Then in 1843, in Boston, Oliver Wendell Holmes attributed the disease to lack of proper precautions about cleanliness by physicians and midwives. Several years later, in Vienna, the young physician Ignaz Semmelweis showed that puerperal fever was a wound infection caused by contamination carried from one patient to another by the examining physician. When he instituted a regimen of hand-washing with a chlorinated solution, the mortality rate at his hospital dropped from nearly 30 percent to about 1 percent. The importance of this procedure was not recognized, however, until the British surgeon Joseph Lister applied Louis Pasteur's work with microorganisms to the problem of how wounds become contaminated and, in 1865, began operating in antiseptic conditions.

You might ask why, if endometritis is due to bacterial contamination of the uterine cavity, it any longer occurs at all. Shouldn't sterile precautions in labor and delivery entirely prevent the disease?

Sterile techniques do reduce the risk that endometritis will occur. But we now know that the infecting bacteria do not have to be brought from outside the patient's body. In fact, the bacteria that commonly inhabit the vaginas of pregnant women are the usual cause of endometritis today.

Because the cervix dilates during labor, a passageway is established from the vagina to the uterus. Even when a cesarean is done before labor starts, the lochia clears a way through the cervix. Bacteria spread upward from the vagina to the uterus in nearly all women during labor and in the first few days after delivery, even in women who have not been touched or examined by a doctor or nurse. But anything that helps bacteria migrate up through the now-open cervix—frequent internal examinations during labor, or internal fetal monitoring, for example—may increase the chances of infection.

Moreover, the site of placental implantation in the uterine wall is, in effect, a large, easily infected wound. And there may be other wounds that bacteria may contaminate—minor lacerations of the cervix or vagina, more serious injuries in the case of a traumatic delivery, and, most important, an incision in the uterine wall if a cesarean is performed. In some cases, material retained in the uterus after delivery—blood and fragments of placental tissue—may provide an optimal environment for the growth of bacteria.

Luckily, the body has natural bacteria-fighting mechanisms that prevent an infection from occurring in most cases. But these defenses may not always be adequate—if the mother is weak or ill or poorly nourished, for example.

Joan had been at an increased risk of contracting endometritis because she had had a cesarean. I explained this when I met with Joan and Tom at Joan's bedside Sunday morning. I examined Joan's uterus by feeling it through her lower abdominal wall; it was far less tender than it had been. She had now been receiving antibiotics for 36 hours. I showed both parents the temperature graph charted in the hospital record. Joan's temperature was still elevated, but it was drifting down; the response to the antibiotics had started.

In some ways, the problems of illness are solved like problems in business. One must first define the problem, then undertake a corrective plan of action. We had identified post-partum endometritis as our complication and had started intravenous antibiotics. But medical solutions to problems are frequently slow and time-consuming and are often more frightening than business problems. We were all very pleased when Joan's temperature became completely normal on Tuesday and her happy and confident spirit returned.

G.G.P.

# Part Nine

&

# Now That Baby's Here

THE PAGES THAT FOLLOW CONSTITUTE A BRIEF GLIMPSE ahead. You may or may not be beset by "the blues"—but you'll find that should it happen, it's perfectly normal and, as Dr. Panter points out, not unlike the letdown following other exhilarating yet stressful events such as holidays.

You'll certainly be concerned from the start about feeding your baby, and you'll probably breast-feed (most women do, these days); basic guidance is offered here, plus both reassurance and precautions on the serious question of possibly conveying other substances to your infant along with nourishment. And you'll learn how your body gradually returns to its normal reproductive cycle, as well as your options in future family planning.

Finally, in an insightful afterword, Dr. Hillard offers, from both professional and personal experience (she is also the mother of two), some observations on preserving the precious memories of your child's day of birth.

# 51. The Postpregnancy Blues

"I don't feel right," Maureen said. "It's a sort of sadness I've had for the past week, and I don't understand it. We had a great day and it was wonderful being together. But when I awoke the next morning, something seemed wrong. All this past week I remembered the happiness, but I still felt depressed."

No, Maureen wasn't describing a postpartum depression, or the "baby blues," although it sounded very similar. She was, as it happens, expressing her feelings after Christmas, the "postholiday blues." We all hear comments like this after special events. Because people describe postholiday blues in terms similar to those they use to describe postpregnancy blues, it is worthwhile to compare the two experiences.

Parents begin to prepare for childbirth from the onset of pregnancy. They read books, speak to friends and to strangers, and take prepared-childbirth and parenting courses.

People also prepare for Christmas long in advance. It's almost like waiting for a due date. And as the time gets shorter, the excitement mounts, with advertisers announcing how many shopping days are left and the newspaper getting heavier and heavier with ads. In pregnancy, one gets the same sense of an impending event when the visits to the doctor are made every week instead of every month.

In both cases, there is a mounting spirit, a desire for perfection, and the thrill of anticipation. As activity intensifies, and the items of the checklists for both events are ticked off, the emotional investment in each is increased.

Special holidays and childbirth are both special, shared family experiences. Both events rightfully encourage hopes and aspirations. There are also expectations that existing problems will be diminished or even solved. The warm, good, loving time of the event often becomes expanded into a fantasy of perfection, which is not likely to persist in the days that follow.

After holidays, people "mourn." They feel disappointed when

they realize that the old family defects, which all normal families have, are still present. They mourn for their loss of shared joys. They mourn, too, their inability to recapture that earlier family life that is subject to the rosy enhancement of memories of one's childhood.

The postpartum mother mourns for the person that she used to be, that happy-go-lucky, unencumbered person of the past. And she also mourns a bit for her loss of that round belly that brought kindly attention from so many people. Of course, her life is further complicated by the demands of the new baby, and by her rapidly changing hormone levels.

When one prepares for a special event, one should prepare for its aftermath, too. Parents-to-be should discuss the postpartum period in advance and formally define their realistic goals. They should make specific plans for the weeks after coming home with a new baby, not just for the birth process itself. I always tell my patient, when I discharge her from the hospital, that within two days she should leave the baby with a babysitter and go out to dinner with her husband, even if she doesn't feel like going out. This is an effective method of reaffirming that your prior relationship still exists.

This normal reactive sadness can be healed by reconnecting with a supportive person, by expressing and exchanging feelings. Postpartum parents should talk with other postpartum parents, just as people should continue to meet and talk with their families and friends after holidays.

I once asked a psychiatric colleague what practical advice he had for people with postholiday blues. He said, "Send them to a psychiatrist so that they can talk about their feelings." He was partially right and partially wrong. Talking about your feelings is excellent. Like postholiday blues, blues after childbirth are relatively common. But they seldon last for more than two weeks or so, and realizing both their normalcy and their temporary nature should also help you cope. If they do linger, my psychiatric colleague's advice should be followed.

G.G.P.

# 52. Breast-Feeding Basics

Breast-feeding is an ideal and natural way to fulfill an infant's nutritional needs. Breast milk also provides the baby with immunological benefits, and breast-feeding is an intimate, together time for a mother and her baby.

Most of my patients breast-feed their children. They independently reach the decision as to whether or not breast-feeding is appropriate for them. They seldom asked me if they should or should not nurse the coming baby. But I am asked many questions about how long to continue breast-feeding.

Last week Liz M. was in my office for a checkup, and she talked to me about weaning. Liz is the 32-year-old mother of a two-year-old daughter. She said, "All the time people say to me, 'Are you still breast-feeding? Why don't you give it up?' But I don't want to stop. I like the feeling at those two feedings a day when Allison is on my breast. It's very special, and I feel so close to her—it's hard to describe. She eats everything—all regular foods—so I know that she doesn't need nourishment. But I know that she likes the feeling. It's the first thing she does when she wakes up and the last thing she does before she goes to bed. Is this abnormal?"

I quickly reassured Liz that there was nothing abnormal about still breast-feeding a two-year-old toddler. In some countries, nursing goes on for many years. I have Japanese colleagues who can remember coming home from first grade in Japan and going to their mothers' breasts.

It is far too impersonal and arbitrary to allow cultural influences to dictate how long you should nurse your baby. You must define your own special situation. Generally, if you are not sure about whether or not to stop breast-feeding, you are not ready to wean your baby.

The appropriate time for weaning will define itself, provided the mother is well-read and well-informed about the subject. Speak to other nursing mothers and to mothers who have nursed in the past so that you may benefit from their experience. Joining a mothers' discussion group is very helpful. La Leche League is an organization devoted to encouraging mothers to breast-feed, and their local chapters will help mothers with specific breast-feeding problems. (A list of chapters can be obtained by writing to La Leche League's main office at 9616 Minneapolis Avenue, Franklin Park, Illinois 60131.)

Many women return to their jobs within one or two months after childbirth, and with them, the question of weaning often arises much earlier.

The breast-feeding mother who is away from her child for more than one or two feedings will feel a progressive fullness of her breasts. This is called *engorgement*. As time passes without engorged breasts being emptied, the breasts will become painful and tender. The mother who wishes to continue to nurse must empty her engorged breasts regularly, or else the milk glands will stop producing milk.

The milk can be pressed out with your fingers, a procedure called *manual expression*, or the breast may be emptied by using a small, inexpensive hand breast-pump. This consists of a funnel, which is placed over the nipple, and a rubber bulb. When the bulb is compressed, suction pulls the milk from the breast, and the unpleasant, overfull feeling goes away almost immediately.

A working mother who continues to breast-feed will usually pump her breasts during lunchtime, or perhaps twice during the workday. But some women may not want to be distracted by engorged breasts during working hours. Or the nature of the job may not allow timely breaks to take care of the engorgement. These mothers will wean after just one or two months of breast-feeding.

Occasionally, a mother will think about ceasing breast-feeding almost as soon as she has started. Louise H. called me three days after going home from the hospital. She sounded dejected and I could hear the telltale sniffles that told me she was crying as she said, "It's not going well. I'm tired all the time. I just can't get any rest. My milk is no good. The baby doesn't like it. I want to stop breast-feeding."

Louise was having postpartum blues. I told her that she

should not make any major decisions while her outlook was distorted by depression. We talked about postpartum blues and we agreed that she would wait one more week before thinking of weaning Matthew. The following week, she said, "I'm so happy that I didn't stop nursing. Everything looks brighter now—I don't have that feeling of being overwhelmed. I think it's going to work out fine."

Sometimes, real problems can arise to cause understandable concern. During the first week at home with her new son, Malcolm, Beatrice S. called me one evening. Her voice sounded very worried. "I felt chills and shaking. I took my temperature, and it's 104. My right breast is swollen and tender. Part of it is red. Should I stop nursing?"

Beatrice had in classic terms described *mastitis*, a breast infection. Mastitis is usually due to bacteria that have gained entrance through an irritated or cracked nipple, although often bacteria may gain entrance through a normal-appearing nipple. Treatment with penicillin usually relieves the irritation within one or two days.

Nursing should *not* be stopped, because the resultant breast engorgement interferes with the blood supply of the breast and keeps the infection active. Infants who continue to nurse suffer no ill effects, and the nursing reduces the engorgement and helps the breast to heal itself.

I told Beatrice to rest in bed, to apply warm compresses to her breast, and to take aspirin to lower her temperature and to reduce the inflammation in the breast. I prescribed penicillin for one week and told her to drink twelve glasses of water a day in order to keep her milk flowing. Not only did I stress that she must continue to nurse in order to help the infected breast to become less swollen but I also told her to use a hand breast-pump on that breast after each feeding in order to be sure that the breast was emptied.

When you decide to wean your baby from the breast—at a time that is right for you and your baby, not imposed by someone else—the best way is to do so gradually. It allows your baby a longer period of adjustment, and the breasts will not undergo painful engorgement. You simply omit one more breast-feeding per day every three or four days and substitute another source of nourishment appropriate to your baby's age. Your baby usually will not notice that the number of breast-feedings is diminishing. It takes about two weeks to go from five breast-feedings a day to none, and you will notice hardly any engorgement in the process.

G.G.P

# 53. Milk—And Maybe More

"My daughter-in-law had decided to nurse her baby. Her obstetrician okayed her decision. Yet, while he was on vacation last week, an associate examined my daughter-in-law and, upon further discussion of breast-feeding, counseled her that since she was on medication for an overactive thyroid, breast-feeding was contraindicated. Whose advice should be followed?"

This was part of a letter I received from an upset mother-in-law, who wondered which advice would be best. The answer is actually easy: Any drug that the mother takes can be looked up in a reference book to see if it is secreted in the breast milk and whether or not it would affect the baby. But there are general principles that are worth discussing.

In order for any drug to appear in breast milk, it must get into the bloodstream of the mother and be transported to the breast glands. The glands, in turn, must pick up the drug and incorporate it into the milk.

The drugs that act or are administered strictly locally, and are not absorbed into the bloodstream, are totally safe. Examples would be drugs in skin creams used for rashes or other skin conditions.

Similarly, while laxatives are drugs that are taken internally, most laxatives stay in the intestines, moving down and acting in a local fashion without being absorbed into the bloodstream of the mother. Examples of locally acting laxatives are milk of magnesia and mineral oil. (Some of the stronger laxatives do get absorbed, however, and can cause the baby to have diarrhea.)

Some drugs that the mother takes are excreted in the breast milk but are destroyed in the infant's stomach by stomach acids and enzymes, whose normal function is to digest the milk. Examples of drugs that the baby destroys by digesting them are insulin, adrenalin, and some other hormones. These would be safe.

Certain drugs can actually appear in breast milk in greater concentration than in the mother's blood itself. This means that even low doses taken by the mother can seriously overdose the baby. Certain tranquilizers are examples of this mechanism, and tranquilizers should not be taken by the nursing mother without specific approval by her physician.

Most mothers are aware of the *obvious* drugs, that is, the prescription medicines they are taking. These might include an antibiotic for an acute illness such as an abscessed tooth, or insulin for diabetes, or birth-control pills. In many cases, though, women don't realize that they may also be taking *non*obvious drugs while they are breast-feeding. Certain vitamins, for instance, if taken in large enough doses, can affect a nursing infant. And over-the-counter medications can be secreted into the breast milk with consequences as serious as those of prescription drugs. Many of our day-to-day habits also introduce drugs into our blood.

Aspirin does enter breast milk, but it is safe for the baby, unless it is taken in high doses over long periods of time. This means that it is quite safe to take two aspirins for a headache.

Caffeine from coffee or tea appears in breast milk only in very low amounts, but the nursing infant excretes the caffeine very slowly. If the mother drinks many cups of coffee, caffeine will accumulate in the baby, and you will notice restlessness and increased excitability. So it's a good idea to limit your coffee to one cup at each mealtime or, better still, to breast-feed first and then have your coffee.

The nursing mother who smokes excretes nicotine in her breast milk. If she smokes heavily—one pack or more per day—the baby can show flushing and excitability as signs of nicotine poisoning, and the milk supply will be reduced also. A nursing mother should smoke very little or preferably, for both her own health and her baby's, stop altogether.

Alcohol is excreted in small amounts in breast milk. Many nursing mothers find that a glass of wine taken before a feeding results in the baby's sleeping longer after that feeding. The mother often believes that the alcohol acts as a "milk punch" to quiet the baby. In reality, though, only small amounts of alcohol appear in the milk, and the alcohol works by calming the mother so that her milk supply is increased and let down more readily. In any event, drink only moderately.

These are merely general guidelines. A nursing mother must be continuously aware of the fact that *anything* she ingests *might* be excreted into her breast milk. This is not a time to be shy about asking your doctor questions about safety.

G.G.P.

# 54. Your Contraceptive Options

After experiencing pregnancy, labor, and the time-consuming demands of mothering a newborn, very few women will choose to have another baby right away. The postpartum period is a good time for a woman to seriously consider the various contraceptive methods available to her.

Granted, spacing children is a very personal decision, but from a medical standpoint, a woman's body needs time to recover from pregnancy—to return to her prepregnancy weight, to build up her iron reserves, and to allow the hormonal levels to get back to normal. And family planning enables couples to make decisions regarding the number and spacing of their children and gives them time to adjust both physically and psychologically to a new child.

Most physicians today no longer feel that the traditional six-to-eight-week postpartum period of sexual abstinence is necessary. When the episiotomy stitches have healed and the lochia, or postpartum discharge, has diminished to spotting, normally by two to three weeks, it is generally safe for a woman to resume sexual intercourse.

She will still be going through physical changes, however, that will affect her sexually. For example, vaginal lubrication with sexual arousal occurs more slowly in lactating women because of decreased estrogen production, and a lubricant may facilitate intercourse.

It is true that breast-feeding helps to prevent pregnancy, but it is not a reliable method of birth control. The return of ovulation after delivery is quite variable, and in breast-feeding women it is often (but not always) inhibited for an even longer period of time. Only about 5 percent of women who are breast-feeding will ovulate by six weeks; about half will ovulate by the fourth postpartum month. But since it is not possible to predict which women will ovulate by six weeks and which will wait for four months or longer, it is impossible to determine who can become pregnant during this time and who cannot.

The contraceptive methods available to a woman during the postpartum period do not differ greatly from those options she has at other times. For some women, abstinence is a practical alternative. For others, methods of birth control need to be discussed so that each woman can make an informed decision based on her medical history, personal needs, and lifestyle.

How effective a contraceptive is in preventing pregnancy depends on many factors. For maximum protection, contraceptives must be used correctly and consistently. The effectiveness of a contraceptive or birth control method is often expressed as a percentage range. The range can be quite wide; the higher figures reflect the method's effectiveness when used properly and consistently, and the lower figures represent the effectiveness in terms of actual experience with the method regardless of whether it was used correctly.

Over-the-counter spermicides, including foams, creams, jellies, sponges, and vaginal suppositories, have the advantage of being easily available without a prescription. The reported failure rates in women using spermicides alone vary widely and reflect careless use as well as the inherent limitations of the products. Research indicates that spermicides are between 70 and 98 percent effective. The risk of pregnancy can be reduced if they are used in combination with condoms.

Spermicides also provide additional lubrication, which some women find advantageous.

Diaphragms and cervical caps are barrier contraceptives and should always be used in conjunction with spermicides. Their effectiveness depends not only on correct and consistent use but also on proper fit and maintenance. A diaphragm must be carefully fitted by a well-trained physician or practitioner and is not available over the counter. The cervical cap is not commonly used in the United States, and the device, which has not yet been approved for general use, is still under study, but the diaphragm has been on the market for many years, and its effectiveness in preventing pregnancy ranges from 83 to 98 percent.

Both methods are of limited usefulness in the immediate postpartum period, however, because the vagina and cervix must return to their normal configurations—a process that usually takes from four to six weeks—before proper fitting can be accomplished. A different size diaphragm is sometimes needed after a pregnancy, and the fit can be checked at the four- or six-week postpartum visit.

Intrauterine devices (IUDs) have been a popular method of birth control and are between 90 and 98 percent effective. Some women should not use IUDs; there are potential complications with them that should be discussed thoroughly with a physician. IUDs are more likely to be expelled if they are inserted immediately postpartum and are thus not inserted until the four- or six-week checkup.

The most widely used reversible method of contraception in the United States is the combination estrogen-progestin pill. In theory, the pill is close to 100 percent effective if taken correctly, and it is generally considered to be a safe contraceptive method for most women. But there are some risks associated with oral contraceptives, including a slightly increased chance of abnormal blood clotting if taken within two weeks after delivery, and it is not the best choice for every woman.

In the United States, oral contraceptives are not generally prescribed for breast-feeding women, although studies have shown that very little of the hormones pass to the baby through the breast milk, especially with the low-dose estrogen pills commonly used today. Estrogens in high doses can suppress lactation, though, and even the low-dose estrogen pills may affect the milk supply if they are taken immediately after delivery. It is best to wait until lactation has been established before taking them. Progestin-only pills (the "minipill"), on the other hand, seem to have little effect on the milk supply; their theoretical effectiveness, however, is slightly lower than that of the combination pills.

Fertility awareness, or natural family planning (rhythm, basal body-temperature method, cervical mucus method, and the sympto-thermal method), is of limited value during the postpartum period. Such factors as breast-feeding, changing hormonal levels, postpartum discharge, and the variability of the return of ovulation can confuse even dedicated and successful users of these methods.

Sterilization is assuming an increasingly important role in family planning. Tubal ligation—cutting, tying, or blocking of the fallopian tubes—is the method of sterilization for women. Since it is generally considered to be irreversible, this method of birth control must be carefully considered. The decision to undergo sterilization should not be made immediately after the intense physical and emotional stress of labor and delivery, and couples should be thoroughly informed about the procedures involved, the risks, benefits, and alternatives.

Selecting a method of contraception should *not* be deferred until the four- or six-week postpartum checkup. Even though the immediacy of the decision may not be apparent until several weeks after the baby is born, every woman should be aware of the options and discuss the various methods with her physician ahead of time, so that she can make an informed and intelligent choice.

P.A.H.

# Afterword:

&#42798;

# Memories of Childbirth

Joan wanted to talk about the birth of her first baby. In fact, she wanted to talk about it to anyone and everyone who would listen. "It was the most wonderful experience of my life," she told her best friend, "to see Anna born, hold her right away, and to have been able to share it all with Bob. I just can't believe what a positive experience it was!"

Joan was going through what has been described as the "taking in" phase, the very early postdelivery period that physicians observe nearly universally. During this time, a woman reviews and remembers the events of labor, incorporating and integrating them into her own personal experience, and shares the associated feelings with close family members or friends.

I believe this is a very important time for a new mother, and I encourage my patients to discuss their labor and birth experiences with their partner or labor coach, the labor nurse, and doctor or midwife. But before the experiences of labor are fully integrated into the memory, the facts should be as accurate as possible. Memory is, after all, not infallible, especially during such periods of intense stress. Misinformation can cause misunderstandings and contribute to negative perceptions of the entire birth experience, so it is best to clarify the events right away.

If you ask most women to describe their labor, they will remember quite a lot about the early stages: where they were when their membranes ruptured, how close together the early contractions were, what they did to try to determine if it was really labor, how they told their partner, and when they decided to call the doctor or go to the hospital. They may remember what the weather was like, what they were wearing, or countless and seemingly insignificant details that serve to anchor the events in reality.

The memories of the events of early labor are often linked to activities of daily living—taking a shower, packing the suitcase for the hospital, resting or sleeping—but these actions may take on special significance because they are associated with the birth of a child. Since contractions during this phase of labor are relatively mild, labor itself does not require a woman's complete concentration.

When the contractions become more intense and regular, however, labor becomes an all-absorbing activity. Particularly during the contractions, women tend to view any distractions as annoying. The laboring woman turns inward for energy and focus, although she appreciates support from a loving partner or caring friend, nurse, midwife, or doctor. It is especially this part of labor that may be remembered in a time-distorted framework, and assistance may be needed later in recalling and sorting out the details of what happened.

Many couples decide that they want to write down all the events of labor so that they can better remember them later on. The events of early labor are often recorded in great detail, with the time and duration of each contraction noted. Later, the records are sketchier, as both husband and wife become more involved with the labor itself. As labor progresses and the contractions intensify, the record-keeping is generally reduced to noting just the major events, such as the times cervical dilation is checked or when medication is requested or administered.

Couples are sometimes surprised when they review these accounts, as they often reveal considerable time distortion. Several hours may be compressed into a few minutes in a woman's memory, or a few minutes may seem like an eternity. For example, the memories that many women have of the transition phase, just before the cervix reaches full dilation, are often described in such statements as, "It seemed as if the contractions were coming with no time in between and lasting forever," when in actuality, this phase of labor is usually relatively short.

Most women remember the second stage of labor as being distinctly different from the first. Instead of relaxing to allow the uterus to do its work, a woman must work with the contractions to push the baby through the birth passage. It demands a much higher level of active participation in the labor process. Some women remember being extremely fatigued or exhausted as the second stage progressed, and they recall needing extra reassurance that labor was indeed progressing, but the memories of the culmination of these efforts—the birth of the baby—usually predominate.

Many women describe the feelings associated with the baby's head crowning as a mixture of pain and elation. The physical sensations of the vagina and perineum stretching are intense, but the emotional high of the immenent birth tends to overshadow the rest. The birth experience itself is frequently remembered and described in superlatives—the best, most wonderful, most intense, most loving time that one could ever experience.

Unfortunately, however, not all birth experiences are good. What if the events of labor and delivery were different from what was expected or anticipated? What if a woman's labor was interrupted by complications for the mother or baby, or if a cesarean delivery was required? In these circumstances, or if the labor was particularly long or difficult, memories of the events can be quite painful. The passage of time, of course, often helps to ease this pain, and if the baby is healthy, that too can help put the memories in perspective.

If, on the other hand, the baby was born with birth defects, or serious medical complications ensued, what was anticipated as a joyous event becomes an occasion for anxiety and concern or sadness. The emotional support of a partner, family members, and close friends is particularly important in helping a woman to deal with these problems, especially during the immediate postpartum period, when physical reserves or strengths have been depleted by labor. The physicians and nurses who work in newborn intensive-care units of large medical centers are usually caring and compassionate individuals who are particularly sensitive to the difficulties experienced by parents in these situations. They can be helpful in contributing support as well as medical care.

Labor is such an intense experience that it can have a certain amnesiac effect by itself, causing events to be incompletely or inaccurately remembered. Some drugs, however, also cause memory distortion. Scopolamine, for example, a drug seldom used in modern obstetrics, induces a "twilight sleep" that many women have found to be an extremely disorienting and disturbing experience, not unlike a nightmare. Narcotics that may be used for pain relief can also produce a "high" or drunken feeling that can affect the way labor is remembered.

Particularly if there were complications during labor, be sure that you ask your doctor to answer any questions about what happened and why; it is especially important that the reasons be understood. It is also best to ask these questions before your memories fade and while the experiences of labor and delivery are still fresh in your mind. Once you have accurate information and understand what happened, you can allow yourself to go on to the next important tasks of loving and caring for your newborn baby.

P.A.H.

# Index

# ABOUT THE AUTHORS

PAULA ADAMS HILLARD, M.D., is an assistant professor of obstetrics and gynecology at the University of Cincinnati Medical Center. She is a contributing editor of *Parents* magazine.

GIDEON G. PANTER, M.D., is an assistant clinical professor of obstetrics and gynecology at the New York Hospital–Cornell Medical Center and practices in New York City. He is a former contributing editor of *Parents* magazine.

Editor DODI SCHULTZ is a medical journalist and a contributing editor of *Parents*. She is co-author with Virginia E. Pomeranz, M.D., of *The Mothers' and Fathers' Medical Encyclopedia*, *The First Five Years* and *From 1 to 2: Your Baby's Second Year*, and is 1985–86 president of the American Society of Journalists and Authors.